Augustine for Armchair Theologians

Also available
in the Armchair Series:

12.71

Augustine for Armchair Theologians

STEPHEN COOPER

ILLUSTRATIONS BY RON HILL

WESTMINSTER
JOHN KNOX PRESS
LOUISVILLE · KENTUCKY

Book design by Sharon Adams
Cover design by Jennifer K. Cox
Cover illustration by Ron Hill

First edition
Published by Westminster John Knox Press
Louisville, Kentucky

This book is printed on acid-free paper that meets the American National Standards Institute Z39.48 standard. ♾

PRINTED IN THE UNITED STATES OF AMERICA

07 08 09 10 11 — 10 9 8 7 6

Library of Congress Cataloging-in-Publication Data is on file at the Library of Congress, Washington, D.C.

ISBN-13: 978-0-664-22372-4
ISBN-10: 0-664-22372-9

Contents

Acknowledgments

I would like to acknowledge a number of individuals who contributed variously to this book: Donald McKim, my patient and helpful editor of the Armchair Theologians series at Westminster John Knox Press; my father, Burton Cooper, who diligently read and edited my draft, making a number of interventions to save me from my wordiness and occasional lapses in taste; and finally, my wife Kabi Hartman and my little girl Eva Emanuela, both of whom have seen somewhat less of me due to my authorial activities.

Stephen Cooper
Lancaster, Pennsylvania
January 2002

INTRODUCTION

Who Is Augustine Anyway?

The name of Augustine evokes the kind of recognition that is generally the mark of great fame or great notoriety. His books, particularly the *Confessions* and *The City of God,* continue to be read. But most of those who know his name have never actually read his writing. Name recognition, however, has its price: Augustine's life is reduced to a caricature in the minds of some. He is given the title of "saint," yet this title can have a negative ring. Those who react favorably to his name tend to regard Augustine the bishop as a model Christian, one who devoted much of his life to the service of God, Christ, and the church. Others receive the name with distaste, as if sensing something unsavory within. Augustine is imaged as an austere and forbidding figure, whose long gaze at the depths of his own sins has led him to look with unsparing eye into the souls of others and convict them harshly of their errors.

This notion of the forbidding Augustine could not be more different from one of his major roles in the history of Christian theology: champion of the grace of Christ, God's redeeming gift to a wayward and recalcitrant humanity. Yet aspects of Augustine's world view are rather foreign to us. Being from a different world and time, Augustine was a man of his own time and world, much as we are children of our own, unfree from the oversights and undersights of our generation. He wrote so many books and commented on so many different areas of life from such a definite point of view that his writings do indeed contain items objectionable to a variety of people for a variety of reasons. The question of his "sainthood," however, is a different matter. For those whose church calls him so, he is a saint. That is not a matter of any one person's opinion.

Whatever our preconceptions about Augustine may be, Augustine is acknowledged all over as a thinker who plumbed the depths of the human soul—although the result is much discussed and sometimes controverted. But one thing is clear: Augustine was a pioneer in territory that Sigmund Freud would later map in his own profound and often hastily dismissed way. Like Freud, Augustine's researches into the recesses of the human mind were stimulated by his own need to come to terms with himself. The *Confessions* is an odyssey of the soul, a story of one person's pilgrimage through this life. Augustine relates his odyssey by a particular type of autobiographical account: a confession, the story of a conversion to God. Interest in Augustine, then, is a sure sign that the question of the self continues to be asked in a theological vein. A theological inquiry into the nature of the self always draws the questioners themselves into question, for to be a self, theologically speaking, means to be a self before God.

Augustine attracts those of us for whom the notion of a universe where one can wander astray and find one's way again has a familiar, if sometimes discomforting, feel. His experiences, quite apart from his intellectual framework, speak a common tongue. If you have ever known the feeling of being lost in the woods or in a strange city, then you also know the relief of finding your way again. The sense of having been lost and then finding one's way again strikes the dominant chord, in a grateful key, of the *Confessions*. The thirteen chapters of this book, which might better be translated as *Conversations*, are the voice of one man's soul to God, a voice simultaneously calling out to other souls who are also before God. In this groundbreaking piece of world literature, Augustine shows us that to be at all means to be from God, to be oriented to God, and to be brought to God by God.

The Relevance of Augustine

O Lord our God, let us abide in hope under the screen of Your wings, protect us and carry us! You will carry us: both as little children and into our graying years You will carry us. For then is our strength really strength, when You are it; but when it is our strength, it is weakness. Our good lives eternally in You; and because we were turned away from there, we have been turned inside out. Let us return now, O Lord, in order not to be overturned, since our good lives in You without any defect, because You Yourself are it. Let us not fear that there be nowhere to return

3

to, since we fell down from there—and while we are not there our home, Your eternity, will not fall down. (*Conf.* IV, 31).

It's well to say "let us not fear" for people firmly convinced of all Augustine says here! But all this may seem a bit much for those of us who struggle to hold on to the notion of God at all, for those of us whose consciousness is weighed down by the ravages of modernity. If we are neither fully able nor fully willing to hear one clear and distinct voice called God, why would the experiences of a Christian bishop of the late Roman world speak to our own? How can his understanding of God, thoroughly conditioned by his historical context, hold much significance for us who are equally if differently encased by our own cultural conditioning? After all, does not our own culture form the medium in which all our linguistic formulations of meaning sink or swim? The elements that separate us from him, spanning the gap of over fifteen hundred years, are legion. Consider, for example, the question of finding commonality between his conversion experience and our own religious experiences. How many of us would jettison our career just when a long-hoped-for success begins to come into view? How many of us would, at the same time, cast away forever the hope of being joined to another human being in that fullest and most intimate of ways? And yet both of these renunciations were part of Augustine's conversion—or part of his decisive conversion to Catholic Christianity, because his was a life that involved more than a few significant turnings.

Paradoxically, Augustine's conversion, foreign as it may be to our own mode of religiousness, is the golden thread that supplies the connection between two very distant and different worlds. For the notion of a conversion, a fundamental change of a whole person through which one becomes different and yet somehow more of one's true self, is a universal experience. We find this kind of experience in many cultures under the auspices of many different religious or philosophical world views. Just as universal, just as truly human, seems to be the desire to communicate that change to others: The changed self reaches out to a curious world in a way that finds—or creates—a ready audience. The very title Augustine gave his greatest work—the *Confessions*—has itself become an exemplar and created a literary genre. The *Confessions of X* is a well-comprehended commodity: Something about X will be revealed in these pages. And what could be more tantalizing than a revelation of someone else's personal life?

But what of Augustine's life can interest us? Most of us

are not headed for a life as a pastor, nor will we write as many books as Augustine or engage in as many theological controversies. So where's the interest? What does Augustine show us that gets our attention, that is worth looking at again and again? I can best answer this question by saying why I read and reread the *Confessions*—and it's not merely because as a college professor I often assign it to my students! Augustine shows us the self in process: the self in doing, or being, now one thing, now the other, in the search for a spiritual identity; and most of all the self as it reflects upon its travelled paths and the ways that lie open in the future. How do I understand why I did what I did? And where was God? Why wasn't I able to see the darkness of my path or the twisting roads that seemed to start straight enough? Did I really have to go the wrong way to get back on the true path? And how was I led astray in the first place, when I just followed a well-worn track?

The Course of His Life

Augustine wandered down a number of different paths before his steps were directed into the Catholic and apostolic church. Any accurate overview of his journey must begin by noting that he was never a pagan. He never worshiped the traditional gods of the cities of the Roman Empire. His father, indeed, was a pagan and maintained the traditional patterns of worshiping these deities: by sacrifice, by public participation on festival days, and so forth. But Augustine was from birth under the stronger tutelage of his mother, Monica. She was a devoted Catholic and eventually won over her less-than-faithful husband to that faith. But whatever their religious differences, Augustine's parents were in total agreement so far as their worldly aspirations for their bright son were concerned. Their boy's intellect had been recognized early on by his teachers; and so his parents destined their son for an academic career that, they hoped, would be a stepping stone to an advantageous marriage and an appointment to a governmental post. Accordingly, they urged their precocious son to excel in his studies. And indeed he did rise from the ranks of his peers, eventually becoming a teacher himself, teaching literature and rhetoric, first in his home town, then in the capital of Roman Africa, thence to Rome, and finally to the imperial capital at Milan. But at the height of his career—an appointment to the official state professorship of Latin rhetoric—he resigned on the grounds of poor health. He had been experiencing strain on his lungs and difficulty breathing. In fact, Augustine's "dropping out" was the result of his religious conversion.

> For You converted me to Yourself so that I no longer went seeking after a wife or any other hope of this world. (*Conf.* VIII, 30).

The path of Augustine's outward success had been attended by some experimenting in the personal realm, in the spheres of both religion and love. But the latter should not be blown out of perspective. Apart from his exceptional performance at school, the young Augustine appears to have had an ordinary childhood. His adolescent sexual adventures, which he refers to with rather chaste allusions, do not seem to have been all that numerous. By the age of seventeen, he was living with a woman who had his son. Only after his mother arranged a socially advantageous match for him did he break up with the woman. A brief relationship with another live-in girlfriend preceded his final conversion to what he conceived to be the full Christian life: a life of celibacy.

His religious searchings and wanderings were certainly more variegated than his sex life. His late teens found him an enthusiastic member of a Christian-gnostic group. The sect of the Manichees saw themselves as the sole possessors of true Christian knowledge and interpretation of the Bible. Other Christians, they maintained, believed absurdities about God and accepted falsified versions of the Scriptures. The young and eager intellect of Augustine was strongly attracted to the complex system of the Manichean religion. The faith of his mother and other Catholic Christians he knew seemed too simplistic for an advanced intellectual like himself. Throw into this mix an interest in astrology, astronomy, and mathematics, and you get the proper perspective on the young Augustine as a seeker of truth. Now imagine that this restless mind is coupled with powerful feelings that manifest in a strong and dominating love of his friends, whom he brings with him throughout the twists and turns of his life. For Augustine conducted his search for wisdom, which he conceived to be a search for true knowledge and the true religion, with other people.

He and his friends read together, talked together, and frequented the Manichees' meetings together. When Augustine finally grew skeptical of this sect's capacity to deliver the truths he sought, he made the time and effort to detach all his friends from their grip.

Where next did this seeker of truth turn? Both to philosophy and to the Catholic (or universal) church. The former offered only relative certainty, with the hope of further revelation of truth. The latter promised him a place of safe-keeping that he had known since his youth. His decisive conversion to the church took place only after a series of events, both inner and outer, that I will detail in this book. He had periods of skepticism and doubt; there was a gradual detachment from past errors, fits of starts and stops. He heard encouraging stories of people who had made tough breaks with the security the world offers. He also deeply read pagan philosophers, who conveyed—if not the whole truth—enough to light the way in the Scriptures held and vouched for by the church. It was in the church that the mature Augustine found his home·and the site of his many labors and numerous books.

This, in brief, is the story of a man whose life and thoughts merit telling and retelling. My aims in this slim volume are modest. I have no pretensions here of feeling out new ground in the sometimes controversial area of Augustinian studies. My goal is to stir up readers whose interests are in the very topics the bishop of Hippo wrote and preached about for more than thirty years. Augustine never tired of writing about God, the soul, and the vocation and destiny of the human being. My presentation of Augustine and his thoughts on these matters will follow his own mode of self-presentation in the *Confessions*. I do this not merely from the sense that Augustine himself chose the extraordinary and groundbreaking literary form of this

work to communicate both his change in life and his theological commitments. Rather, I take my lead from Augustine because I believe that his theology, a theology of grace, develops from a specific story—his story—of being set free. And Augustine's story, of which I can offer only a small part, is a story of seeking, a seeking in life, a seeking in himself, and a seeking in and through books. Now, this is something he has himself told in an incomparably rich fashion. What I can do here is to let him speak for himself as much as possible. Toward that end, I will translate his Latin with a concern both for faithfulness to the original and for expressiveness in our contemporary parlance.

The story I tell about Augustine contains several intertwining stories. There will be a story of losses: lost loves, lost hopes, lost ambitions, lost friends and family. Yet it will also be a story of finding: of finding that you have lost your way and of finding your way, which is the way God has made for you—a narrow way in the wilderness of sin that is at the same time a way out and a way to God.

> It is one thing to see the peaceful homeland from on top of a wooded hill and not to find the path that leads to it, trying in vain to make one's way over impassible ways surrounded by lurking and plotting fugitive deserters with their chief the lion and the dragon. It is another thing to keep to the path that leads in that direction, a path guarded under care of the heavenly emperor where those who have deserted the heavenly army cannot engage in highway robbery. (*Conf.* VII, 27)

CHAPTER ONE

Faint Beginnings

Aurelius Augustinus was born in 354 of the current era (d. 430), the oldest son of a small landholder, who was a respectable citizen of a North African town, Thagaste. Thagaste was located in what the Romans called Numidia Proconsularis (Souk-Ahras in present-day Algeria) and lay about forty-five miles inland from the Mediterranean coast. Augustine's father Patricius (Patrick, as we would call him) was by no means a wealthy man, but he owned enough land to support his family, to have several slaves, and to have aspirations for his son to go beyond his own status. Augustine's mother, Monica, would play a far larger role in his life than his father. She came from a family of modest means. Still, Augustine's family was not poor. They did not belong to the level of population that constituted the vast majority of the Roman Empire (90 to 95 percent of the populace), who were poor farmers. Historians have estimated that fewer than 10 percent of the inhabitants of the late Roman Empire could read, and fewer could write. That Augustine's family provided him with an education at all suffices to say that he was better off than the many, though nowhere near the comfort of the Roman elite.

In terms of what we would called cultural or ethnic identity, Augustine and his family were Roman-African: Roman because of their mother-tongue, Latin; African because of their geographical location in Roman Africa. But when speaking of Roman Africa or Roman Africans, we need to provide distance from our present day racial and geographical associations. "Africa" was what Romans called the province (Africa Proconsularis) whose capital was Carthage, the Phoenician colony planted in the eighth century B.C. along the North African (southwestern) Mediterranean coast. Carthage was an important commercial sea-faring power in the ancient world, which Rome finally destroyed after the long series of Punic wars of the third and second centuries B.C. Later the Romans resettled the area with army veterans, and Africa became just another part of the Roman Empire in which local peoples and traditions were incorporated to various degrees in the culture of the Roman world. Other Romans thought the African Romans had a peculiar accent and considered them passionate in their emotional life—or at least this was the stereotype. The name of Augustine's mother, "Monica" (or rather, Monnica, in his spelling), is not a Latin name but is probably Berber, coming from a local deity named Mon. From this some scholars have suggested she may not have been altogether of Roman origin. Whatever the case, we can be sure that Augustine and his family identified with the Latin culture of the long-settled conquerors, not the strata of the populace who still spoke Punic (a language related to Hebrew), or even Berber, an African language spoken in the countryside, as it still is in some parts of Algeria today.

The opening of the *Confessions* does not supply us with the kind of concrete, personal information, that we would expect in a sketch of a life. Rather, its first lines get to the matter closest to Augustine's heart: an address to God as a Life whose nature, markedly different from our own, cannot be wholly captured in thought. Augustine considered the essential facts about himself somewhat incidental to the point of his book. When we call the *Confessions* an autobiography, we are using the term in the broad sense of "self-writing," rather than the usual, more restrictive meaning. The book is not, at any rate, a comprehensive account of the facts of his life.

> You are great, O Lord, and very worthy of praise: Your power is great and Your wisdom is beyond measure [see Psalms 48:1 and 14:5]. Humanity, just a little bit of Your creation, wants to praise you, to praise you even as it carries around its own morality, carries around a witness to its sin, a witness that You oppose the proud. Yet humanity, just a little bit of Your creation, wants to praise You. You stir us up so that it would delight us to praise You, since You made us for Yourself and our heart is uneasy till it is at ease in You. Grant me, O Lord, to know and understand what comes first: to call on You or to praise You? Or does knowing You come before calling on You? But does anyone call on You unknowingly? (*Conf.* I, 1)

Scholars looking into the motivations for this work point to a number of factors. On the one hand, Augustine needed to explain to the church who he was now in light of his Manichean past. For although he was now a Catholic bishop, many Latin Christians of his day, particularly in Africa, knew him as a heretic. Another impetus to write the *Confessions* was as a response to a rather well-known (and very well-to-do) Christian ascetic and scholar, Paulinus of Nola. Augustine's friend Alypius had opened a correspondence with Paulinus, who wondered how it was that Alypius had converted to the ascetic life. Alypius seems to have passed the question on to Augustine. This may explain why in his own conversion narrative he gives ample space to Alypius's biography and conversion. But the various external circumstances that contributed to the work are just that: contributing circumstances. It was the driving force of Augustine's own mind and spirit that brought him to this project. His own spiritual experience led him to give expression to a new and deeper understanding of St. Paul's teaching on divine grace. And his new understanding was something that had developed during the decade after his conversion to the Catholic church. Those were the years in which his attempts to work over his past percolated in his mind with his growing knowledge of the Bible and his experience of the life of faith.

First and foremost, however, the book is the story of a spiritual journey. In its own time, there was nothing odd about the fact that the *Confessions* lacked a self-centered autobiographical introduction. In this regard it reminds us of the opening of the earlier biography of the philosopher Plotinus. This great pagan thinker of the previous century exercised a significant influence on the conversion and thought of Augustine. Plotinus, the founder of Neoplatonism, was—according to his student and biographer

Porphyry—extremely reticent about the factual data of his life; Augustine too seems to have wanted to direct his readers to the spiritual aspect of his life.

This is certainly the impression we get from Book I of the *Confessions*. After the opening address to God, Augustine goes on to speak of his infancy and his early boyhood in schools. But he is in no sense just giving us facts. The "facts" of his infancy are couched within questions. These questions, which are spiritual in nature, lie dormant in the facts themselves, requiring a great thinker to bring them to speech.

> What is it that I want to say, O Lord, except that I don't know from where I came here into this—how shall I say it—this deathly life or living death? I don't

know. But the consolations of Your mercies took me up, as I have heard from the parents of my flesh, from which and in which You formed me in time—for I myself don't remember. So the consolations of human milk took me in: but it wasn't my mother or my nurses who filled their breasts for themselves. Rather, for the sake of my infancy, it was in accordance with Your institution that through them You gave me nourishment, even the riches laid up at the base of things. In addition, you gave me not to want more than what You gave; and to those nursing me You gave them to want to give to me what You were giving them. According to a preordained feeling, they wanted to give to me what they were overflowing with from You. For the good I got from them was a good for them—and it was not a good from them but through them. Obviously, O God, all things are from You: from my God as well comes all health and salvation to me. This fact came to my attention later, when You cried out to me through those very things, which You supplied inside and out. For as a baby I knew how to nurse and to rest content in what pleased me, but to weep at the ailments of my flesh, and I knew nothing more. (*Conf.* I, 7)

Augustine describes his infancy in terms that could apply equally to all human beings. In our beginnings we find ourselves placed in a context of givenness: Other people are given to want to give us what we need. As a baby, Augustine stood in need of certain basic goods that were simple; and it was a good for the others to give what had been given them. Yet tears there must be, when the adult judgment of what is good comes into conflict with the limited view granted babies! Augustine also asks a deeper question. Where does the life of an individual come from? Must it not come from somewhere? Schooled in modern science, we may automatically reject any notion of the soul's pre-existence. Although we rightly associate the idea of reincarnation with Hinduism and Buddhism, many people today believe in reincarnation apart from any relation to those religions. In the early church, some Christians speculated about whether souls existed before coming into bodies. Nor were all these thinkers of heretical stripes. Most of these theologians would have wanted to be considered mainstream and orthodox. Platonist philosophy had certainly influenced these Christian thinkers; but there were also Jews before the time of Christ who had entertained this possibility.

For Augustine, any talk of the beginning of life—human life—must also involve mentioning life's end. He regarded the beginning of our mortal life in the flesh as a beginning with death, because life in the flesh always involves the death of the flesh. Is our existence—he asks, with a serious word-play—a "deathly life or living death"? Our mortal body, unlike the future resurrection body, is a sign of the death that accompanies us pace by pace in this life. Due to the link between death and sin in the story of Adam and Eve, Augustine refers to our being wrapped in "the testimony of our sin." Thus we wear our mortal state upon our sleeves (only youth is spared this vision). The view may seem gloomy, but it is not, at least for Augustine. He is assured, and assures us that human beings will be clothed by God with immortal bodies—that is, those of us who come under God's grace. The reign of life, then, if it triumphs over death—reckoned by many as the most dreadful of all things—may also extend backward. Might there not also be life before earthly life? One may at least ask whether God is continually creating new souls or whether there is a reservoir of already created souls.

Prior to Augustine, and perhaps exerting an influence

on him, were several Neoplatonic-thinking Christians who speculated about the pre-existence of the soul. They thought of the soul as existing as a bodiless spirit before its incarnation—or incarceration—in a physical body, which came about as a result of a fall. Along this line of thinking, the physical world and the human body were created as a penalty for sins, a training ground for exercise in virtue, in order to enable souls to return to a pure spiritual state. Thus chastened, they would be wiser for their experience. We find this view held by Marius Victorinus, a philosopher and teacher of rhetoric whose conversion Augustine recounts in the *Confessions*. Victorinus wrote the first Latin

commentaries on St. Paul, which Augustine may have read. In his comments on Ephesians 1:4 ("just as he chose us in Christ before the foundation of the world . . ."), Victorinus suggests that all souls pre-existed in Christ before the world had been created. So it's not out of the question that Augustine may have held the same view or at least entertained it as a serious suggestion. Indeed, a number of passages in the *Confessions* hint at speculations in this direction.

> Tell me, God, did my infancy follow upon some other age of mine now dead? Or is it merely the one I passed in my mother's womb? I have received reports about that age, and I myself have seen pregnant women. Was there something before this age as well, my Sweetness, my God? Was I anywhere or anything? For I have no-one who could tell me such things: neither my father nor mother were able, nor was the experience of others and my own memory any help. You're not laughing at me, are You, when I'm asking these things . . . Where does any living creature such as this come from if not from You, Lord? (*Conf.* I, 9–10)

Even if this strikes us as a bizarre and novel notion for a Christian, there is something profound in raising this question of where we were before this life. Not knowing where we come from in the fullest sense of the term, we are forced to acknowledge that our existence is grounded in a mystery. This mystery is ultimately unfathomable, no matter how much science unravels the processes of our beginnings. Reduce us to an egg and a sperm, if you like, and to the DNA in them, but what comes before that? and before that? And so on to infinity. What's more, how we work on a biological level does not tell us why we exist or what our purpose is. That is a question of a different order and requires its own mode of discourse.

Augustine argues here that our very existence is something given to us in such a manner that a giver beyond our physical parents must be assumed. He points out that even the means by which we are nourished—and the fact that we "instinctively" know how to take that nourishment—are given. Call it nature, call it instinct, call it what you will, but look at it in light of the mystery that Augustine sees revealed in these everyday things. These everyday things conceal the riches of the Giver—God—at their base. This kind of vision is for those whose eyes have been spiritually opened. Only then can we see what is not apparent to the naked eye, which sees only the outside of things. In order to really see, says Augustine, we need faith.

Among the givens Augustine believes we get from God is a basic orientation to the life of the senses. This sensory knowledge is clearly related to our ability to survive. As an infant, Augustine remarks, he already knew the goods and evils of bodily comforts and discomforts. He will never deny that these are real goods and real evils. But there are other goods besides the goods of the senses; there are the goods of the spirit. The big question for human beings is whether we rank the goods and evils of the senses in the proper order among all the goods. One further point in Augustine's discussion of infants indicates his sharply observant eye: He notes that an infant's sense of humor develops before speech does.

> Later I began also to laugh, first while sleeping and then while awake. This fact about myself was reported to me and I believed it, since we see the like in infants other than ourselves—for I don't recall this part of my life. And look: gradually I came to an

awareness of where I was; and I wanted to make my desires known to those by whom they could be fulfilled. But I was incapable of doing this, because my desires were inside but those people were outside, and they didn't have the capacity in any of their senses to enter into my soul. So I tossed around both limbs and noises as signs similar to my desires, the few signs that I could make—not that they bore any true similarity. And when I was not obeyed (whether because I was not understood or because it would have been harmful), I became indignant with the grown-ups who were not subservient to me, even with the free people who would not serve me; and I avenged myself upon them by howling. I have learned that all babies, whom I've been able to learn from, are like this. That I was also like this, the babies themselves unknowingly reported to me better than my nurses who did know me. (*Conf.* I, 8)

Here's the paradox of human existence as Augustine has formulated it. Babies struggle to survive by all means necessary. Their general helplessness makes them often angry

23

and causes them to act in ways that adults would regard as unjustifiable, except for their ignorance. But their weakness is not, for Augustine, a good reason to consider them free of guilt. "It is the weakness of infants' limbs that makes them harmless [or "innocent," as the Latin could just as well be translated], not their intention." This was another thing that Augustine learned from babies he observed. "I myself have seen and had experience of a jealous child: still without speech, he, pale with anger looked upon his fellow-nursling with a bitter face." This cannot be called innocence, this unwillingness to share an abundant flow of milk with another child who would surely die without it. Mothers and nurses, Augustine notes, claim to know how to wean out such tendencies by some mysterious remedies; but the tendencies, which themselves can hardly be overlooked or called slight, are tolerated only because they are destined to vanish with age.

These observations concerning childhood seem to have fed into Augustine's question about whether we in any sense existed before our birth. His observations on the nascent evils of the childish mind fit with what he read in parts of the Bible. For it contains sayings from which he would later formulate his understanding of the doctrine of "original sin." Augustine's thoughts on this subject were of vital importance to the development of Protestant theology. Reformation theologians like Luther and Calvin followed Augustine's lead in regarding the fallen nature of humankind as a signal reason why God's grace not only forgives but heals and rehabilitates us from the damage all humanity incurred by reason of the first sin.

> Because, if I was conceived in iniquity and my mother nourished me in sins in her womb [see Ps. 51:5], where or when, O Lord, was I Your servant ever innocent?

But look, I'll pass over that time—how can a time I have no memory of concern me now? (*Conf.* I, 12)

Augustine moves on to describe his growth from infancy to boyhood and particularly his early experiences. He observe that speech, the most important skill, did not need to be taught. "For the grown-ups did not teach me by setting out words in a certain order of instruction, as was the case shortly thereafter with reading. Rather I myself by the mind you gave me, O my God, with grunts, various noises, and various motions of my limbs, I would seek to bring out the thoughts of my heart in order that my desires would be obeyed." That learning which seemed to come by itself Augustine contrasts with what took place at school. Sent there by adults "that I might be successful in this world and excel in skillful speech to get honor among people and riches that deceive those who chase after them," he was

threatened with corporal punishment if he did not devote himself to his studies. It was fear of the rod that first brought little Augustine to prayer.

> For as a boy I began to pray to You, my Help and my Refuge. I was untying the knots of my tongue; and as a little boy I prayed to You with no little emotion that I would not be beaten in school. And when you did not heed me . . . those blows, that great evil which weighed heavily upon me then, were laughed at by the grown-ups, even by my parents themselves who did not wish any evil to happen to me. . . . Could there be anyone, who by sticking to You so reverently would be so great-minded that he would reckon racks, hooks, and other similar instruments of torture to be no big deal? To escape such things, people beseech You with great fear throughout the whole world. We neither feared our punishments less nor prayed less to avoid them; and yet we were sinning by not writing, reading, or learning our letters as much as was demanded of us. There was no lack, O Lord, of memory or brain power, which You wanted us to have sufficiently for our age—but it delighted us to play. And this was avenged upon us by those who were certainly doing such things themselves. But the games of adults are called business. (*Conf.* I, 14–15)

Despite his fears of being beaten, Augustine admits to having shirked his studies due to his love of play. Looking back he finds it ironic that children are punished for their love of playing when those who punish them delight in their own kinds of play just as much. How different from a child angry at losing a ball game was a professor hot under the collar at a colleague who had gotten the better of him regarding some picayune point?

Augustine's criticism of his schooling and certain features of the adults who set the program tells us early on that his book consists of more than just confessions of sin and praise to God. The *Confessions* contains criticisms of all the human institutions that accomplish what we would call socialization. He critiques the educational curriculum of the day because the literature which formed its basis taught quite different lessons than the schoolmasters and parents intended. Great literature contains all sorts of characters, not all of them salubrious. But Augustine was worried about the moral effect of literature. Moreover, the element

of fear was never absent. The teacher's rod was always there to back up the demand for diligence in studying. At home, chaste conduct was taught by Augustine's mother, and no doubt by other mothers as well, backed up with threats of all sorts.

> But woe unto you, O river of human custom! Who can resist you? How long will you continue to run? How long will you tumble Eve's children into the huge and fearsome ocean, which those who embark on the wood of the cross barely cross over? Didn't I read in you of Zeus both thundering in judgment and committing adultery? Clearly he could not consistently do both of these; yet it was written so that real adultery could have an authority to imitate, while the fake thundering plays the pimp. But which of our robed professors can breath easily when he hears one of his chalk-dusted fellows saying this out loud: Homer made these things up and ascribed human qualities to the gods, though I would prefer he had ascribed divine qualities to humans? But one would more truly say: that poet did indeed make these things up, but he did so in order that crimes not be considered crimes through his associating divinities with human beings and their criminal deeds. The result is that anyone who had done these things would seem to be an imitator, not of people lost in error, but of the heavenly gods. (*Conf.* I, 25)

Augustine rejects the argument that this racy literature is necessary for students to read for the sake of expanding their vocabulary: "No way, no way are these kinds of words learned more easily by means of their filthy context, rather is this kind of filth perpetrated more confidently by means of these words." And here again the fault belongs with the teachers, who refuse to acknowledge their double standard. "It's not the words I'm bringing charges against—they are like choice and expensive vessels—rather it's against the wine of error which is served in them to us by the drunken teachers. And unless we drank, we were beaten—and no appeal was permitted to any sober judge." (Following the manner of biblical prophets, Augustine uses the words "wine" and "drunken" to describe the senseless conduct of people who are otherwise quite sober.)

Augustine's criticisms of his schooling, of course, come from the mouth of one who excelled in schools beyond most of his peers. It's as if the captain of a high school football team, who went on to college on a football "scholarship," were lamenting the role of sports in public education. Rarely do people criticize the thing through which they got their name, fame, and money. Yet this is what our changed person is doing in the *Confessions*. Augustine tells us that he was selected by his grammar teacher to perform an exercise that was an important part of learning the language arts. This exercise involved taking a passage of poetry, rephrasing it in prose, and pronouncing it aloud with feeling and appropriate gestures. In this case his teacher set him the task of doing this exercise with a portion of Virgil's *Aeneid* where the queen of the gods, Juno, rages because she is not permitted to deny Aeneas a safe landing in Italy. Augustine describes that task as "a matter of anxiety for his soul," something done under "the promised reward of praise or in fear of shame and blows." At the time he may have felt special, honored, singled out—even if he did experience anxiety about performing well enough to make his parents proud. But when as a bishop he looks back on this event, his feelings are quite different. He shows a critical and discerning spirit, one unwilling to accept human convention and the easy "that's just the way it's always been done" rationale.

What is going on here? I, the queen of the gods, am unable to prevent this Trojan king from landing in Italy to set up a new kingdom? The Fates won't permit me to prevent it, they say! What's up with that? Didn't Athena get to vent her rage against the Greeks and sink their ships just because of the crimes of one of their soldiers, Big Ajax? And I can't do anything against Aeneas? This world is topsy-turvy, not to be endured! (Virgil, *Aeneid,* I, 38)

But what was the point of this for me, O my God, my true life? Why the cries of approval to me when I recited this in the presence of my peers and fellow students? Look—wasn't this all smoke and wind? So there wasn't anything else on which my mind and tongue could have been exercised? Your praises, O

> Lord, Your praises found throughout Your scriptures
> would have upheld my tender growing heart, so it
> would not have been uprooted by empty trifles as
> filthy plunder for flying creatures. For it is not just in
> one way that sacrifice is made to the fallen angels.
> (*Conf.* I, 27)

Augustine finds fault with both the substance and the
style of his schooling, even if it was the ticket to a successful career. Augustine is engaging in social criticism from a
theological perspective. The pattern of a sinful or wayward
life is not just an individual thing, not just a path we choose
to embark on of our own. Rather, Augustine wants to
show us that human society as a whole, precisely through
its approved institutions, casts the children into a "river of
human custom" and then becomes worried—hypocriti-
cally—when the children show all the corruption of the
adult ways. "Now what wonder was it that I was carried off
thus into meaningless things and was going far off from
you, my God," when the men set out to him as role models were more upset by grammatical mistakes than they
were by their own rotten deeds?

Let us not think, however, that Augustine is criticizing
only pagan society. In a revealing incident about a time in
his childhood when he became deathly ill, he shows us that
Christians too perpetuate customs that are in tension with
religious truth. This little story of his sickness is very important for establishing that Augustine was brought up as a
Christian and had a conscious identification with that faith.

> While still a boy I had heard about the eternal life
> promised to us through the lowliness of our Lord
> God who came down to meet our haughtiness; and I
> was marked with the sign of the cross and seasoned
> with salt at the moment I came from my mother's

31

> womb who put much hope in You. You saw, O Lord,
> that although I was still a boy, becoming feverish on
> a certain day with a stomach pain and about to die—
> you saw, O my God, since You were already my
> guardian, with what emotion and what faith I
> demanded the baptism of Your Christ from the devo-
> tion of my mother and that of the Mother of us all,
> Your church. (*Conf.* I, 17)

His mother fearfully and diligently made preparations to
have him baptized. She was a Catholic Christian and
believed that this sacrament would cleanse her son of his
youthful sins, allowing him to enter the peace of all the
saints in case his fever carried him off. The boy, however,
recovered, and the ceremony was deferred. Augustine tells
us the grounds for this deferral: "if I were to live, I would
become still more soiled, since the guilt contracted in the
soilings of transgressions after that washing was going to
be great and more dangerous." His mother's decision to
put off his baptism was not uncommon among Christian
parents of the time. Augustine's father was not yet a Christian, but his mother struggled "so that you, my God,
would be father to me, rather than that man." People back
then regarded baptizing a child as a risky proposition,
because once it was done, how would future sins be
washed away? Yet it was precisely this kind of calculating on
the part of his pious mother that disturbs Augustine as he
looks back on the whole incident.

> I beg you, my God, I would like to know—if you too
> would like me to know—what was the plan that held
> me back from getting baptized at that time? Was it
> good for me that the reins of sin were loosened, as it
> were? Or were they not loosened? Where does it come
> from that even now talk reaches our ears from every-

where about this or that person: "allow him, let him do it—he's not yet baptized." But when it comes to the welfare of our body we don't say "let him be further damaged, for he isn't yet cured." So how much better if I were cured quickly, and if it were accomplished for me through my own diligence and through that of my family, so that the health of my soul were guarded by Your guardianship, which you had bestowed. Indeed it were better. But how many great waves of temptation seemed to loom over me once childhood was over! This mother had taken note of them already, and she wanted to commit to them the raw material out of which I would later be formed, rather than the formed image itself. (*Conf.* I, 18)

Given what Augustine has told us about himself, nothing entitles us to regard this as the first chapter in the life of a great sinner. The sins of his infancy, which give rise to such great speculations, are the sins of all babies; and the transgressions of his early childhood couldn't be more normal—the occasional pilfering from his parents' pantry to feed his growing appetite and a neglect of his school-work due to a preference for play! The regrets he expresses about this part of his life are regrets concerning matters beyond his control: the reading material and the conduct of the teachers at school; his mother's deferral of his baptism. If we look at Augustine's main regret about his own performance in this period, it in no way implies he saw himself as an extraordinary sinner. His experiences simply show that human nature prefers a path sweetened with tasty delights rather than a rocky road whose traversal eventually leads to a great prize. "Now what was the reason why I hated learning the Greek language, in which I was immersed as a small boy? Even now this question has not been probed to my satisfaction."

The details Augustine supplies about his education are of great interest to scholars of late antiquity, the period of the Roman Empire beginning from the late third century A.D. While Roman education in the age of Caesar and Cicero included both Latin and Greek, by Augustine's time it was a rare Latin speaker who had command of the tongue in which so much philosophy, history, and science was written. Yet a knowledge of Greek continued to be part of the ideal of Roman education and culture. At Augustine's school, Greek was diligently taught, although not diligently studied even by bright students like him. His laziness in Greek set him off on a line of inquiry about certain aspects of human nature. Why was it that he loved the stories of Latin literature found in Virgil's great epic *The Aeneid*, whereas he hated to learn Greek? Mastering Greek would have opened him to the joy of Homer's great epics.

"One can clearly see that the difficulty, the difficulty in every way of learning a foreign language, sprinkled gall—as it were—into the entire sweetness of the fabulous Greek stories." The adult Augustine regretted his failure to have applied himself in his youth to the Greek lessons. Although he had learned enough to compare the authoritative Greek of the Bible with the Latin translation then in use, he hadn't the ability to read important philosophical or theological works in Greek. Later, however, the press of theological controversy forced him to bone up on his Greek to consult a medical treatise on some technical matters of biology relating to the transmission of original sin. He attributes his neglect of the language in his early school years not only to the difficulty of learning those first rudiments of the language—a difficulty quickly overcome in the case of Latin, his mother tongue—but also to his love of the stories Latin gave him easy access to. It is instructive how he depicts this early error. His failure to crack down and memorize all those Greek verb and noun forms arose not from any evil lust or love of evil but from the love of another "good": the stories found in the Latin literature that so enchanted his soul.

Augustine describes his early failings as betrayals of God. This may strike us as peculiar. It is hard for us to imagine a kid today presenting his involvement with the characters in a story as tantamount to religious infidelity. Yet this is what we hear from Augustine.

> For what is more miserable than a miserable wretch who, failing to commiserate with himself, nonetheless weeps for the death of Dido—which happened by her loving Aeneas—and doesn't weep for his own death, which happened by not loving You, O God, the light of my heart, the bread of my soul's inner mouth and

the power that weds my mind and the deep recess of my thoughts? I wasn't loving You, rather I was fornicating away from You [see Ps. 73:27 KJV]; and to me in my fornication voices rang out all around: "Well done, well done!" For the friendliness of this world is fornication away from You; and "well done, well done" is said to the point that one is ashamed not to be that way. This I did not weep about; I wept about Dido, "who pursuing her furthest end died by a sword" [Virgil, *Aeneid,* VI, 457]. I myself was pursuing Your furthest creatures, having abandoned You;

> as earth I was going to earth. Were I prohibited from
> reading these things, I would mourn, as then I would
> not be reading material to mourn over. Madness of
> this sort is regarded a part of language better and
> richer than those language arts by which I learned to
> read and write. (*Conf.* I, 21)

Why does Augustine as an adult interpret these minor childhood infractions as "fornication" against God? The use of the word "fornication" to refer to non-sexual sins may be particularly confusing for us. Augustine employs the term in the way the Old Testament prophets (especially Hosea, Jeremiah, and Ezekiel) did: to mean idolatry, or devotion to another god besides the God of Israel who made the universe. Because as a boy he loved aspects of the creation more than God, he saw himself as committing idolatry, spiritual fornication against God. Thus he interprets his reaching for the delights of creation, including human works of art, as distancing himself from God. And that cannot be good.

This desire to be on one's own is for Augustine the fundamental aspect of human sin. Sin, as a quality of our actions, comes to qualify our whole existence. As such, sin is a state of being, or rather—because our lives are movement—sin is a kind of existence in which we seek to find ourselves apart from God. For this reason, Augustine loved the parable of the prodigal son. This figure appears throughout the *Confessions* as the image for all humanity who, searching for themselves and seeking to make their own lives by themselves, get farther and farther from God. This human prodigality is part of our spiritual condition. We move away from the only true source of nourishment. Still, for Augustine, although this is a movement in the wrong direction, it is nonetheless a movement of the mind

in relation to its perceived goods. Yet there is clearly a problem with our perception.

> I was far off from Your face in my darkened disposition. For not by means of one's feet or distant places does one depart from You and return to You. Nor indeed did that younger son of yours look for a horse, a carriage, or a boat, nor did he fly away on a visible wing or make his way by moving his legs in order to live in a distant land and prodigally waste what You had given to him as he set out. You were a sweet father to him because You had given him his share; and when he returned full of need, You were sweeter still. So it was in a condition of craving—a darkened condition—that he set out, and that state was far from Your face. (*Conf.* I, 28)

In his retrospective look at himself, Augustine reads the story of his life, so to speak, in light of the parable of the prodigal son (Luke 15:11–32), and this is how he presents it for his readers. The entirety of the *Confessions*, indeed, can be read as a meditation on the human departure from God, and on the distance between God and human beings even after they had made their way home to be embraced by Mother Church and a loving father. The insight with which Augustine ends his first chapter is couched in the form of a prayer and contains a thanksgiving and a petition, both of which reveal the first principle of what will be a fully developed theology of grace: "Thanks be to You for Your gifts, but may You preserve them for me. For thus will You preserve me, and the gifts which You have given me will be increased and completed; and I will be with You, since You have also given me my existence."

CHAPTER TWO

Teenager in Love

The second book of the *Confessions* reveals a sixteen-year-old Augustine returning home after having spent a year in Madaura, a nearby city where he had gone to study rhetoric. His parents had now expended their meager resources for his schooling, so the youth found himself with a year off in which to get in trouble. Augustine offers only a general sketch of this period, but he uses that account to develop several lines of questioning on important theological issues. A key feature in his life at that point was a longing, a lust even, for experiences to boast about among his group of friends. However, the specific incident that provides the real jumping-off point for his theological reflection on sin turns out to be not sexual lust but a theft he and his friends committed.

However large sex loomed in Augustine's life at this time, it is not presented in the *Confessions* as the root of sin. But it does serve as an excellent example of what sin is all about. This realm of life, he thinks, is a tinder-box of sin, definitely something to be approached with caution. Thus Augustine alerts his readers to his reasons for recounting his adolescent lusts. Neither to titillate his readers nor to give himself a sweet remembrance of old pleasures now long renounced, Augustine relates his sins to make God's merciful nature known and to acknowledge what he, a former sinner, now is.

> I want to recollect my bygone filthy deeds, the fleshly corruptions of my soul, not because I love them but so that I might love You, my God. For love of Your love I'm doing this sort of thing, recalling my wicked ways in the bitterness of my examination so that You might become sweet to me, a sweetness that is not false, a sweetness happy and secure, one which gathers me up from the dispersion in which I was cut apart for naught. Turning away from You who are One, I lay waste among many things. For at that time of my youth, I burned to be satiated with hellish things. I even dared to grow wild with various shadowy loves. My beauty faded away, and I became putrid in Your eyes, pleasing myself and desiring to please human eyes. And what was it that delighted me but to love and to be loved? (*Conf.* II, 1)

Passages like this are probably the reason for the mistaken impression that Augustine was once a terrible sinner, a man who sinned beyond his peers and was now horribly guilt-ridden, though still inclined to describe the sins of his youth in lurid language. This misreading is understandable, because it is occasioned to a great degree by the style of writing that was popular during Augustine's day. Audiences in the ancient Mediterranean world appreciated and enjoyed flowery and overblown language. How many of us nowadays would refer to our adolescent sexual experimentations as "filthy deeds" or "fleshly corruptions of my soul"? But there was nothing exceptional about his behavior according to the standards of that day. Augustine records his father's typical and lusty reaction when they went to the baths together. Patrick saw signs that made him think that grandchildren would not be long off: "rejoicing, he made the fact known to my mother, rejoicing in the excess of drink in which this world of Yours— drunk from the invisible wine of its own will that is twisted and bent upon the lowest things—forgets You its Creator and loves Your creation in place of You." That Augustine's father had become a catechumen (having succumbed to the silent pressure of his wife) and was preparing for baptism clearly did not change his old habits of mind!

Augustine criticizes not only his father's worldly mindedness; his saintly mother also comes in for some hard questions. Why didn't she arrange an early marriage for him that would have held his lust within lawful bounds? Her attitude was not the same as her husband's—the man-to-man, nudge-nudge, wink-wink sensibility. No, as Augustine tells us, "she admonished me with great concern that I not have sex and most of all that I not commit adultery with any man's wife." To which Augustine, the red-blooded teenager, responded: "these admonitions seemed womanish to me, and I would have been ashamed to have heeded them."

So she was shaken with a devoted trepidation and fear; and although I was not yet baptized, she was still worried about the twisted ways in which those people walk who "put their back toward You and not their face" [Jer. 2:27]. (*Conf.* II, 6)

Why didn't Augustine's mother just marry him off and avoid all the anxious concern? There would have been nothing unusual or abnormal in this, and one would think it more in the character of her faith. But Augustine's parents, like the rest of us, were not motivated by faith alone. "There was no concern on the part of my parents to pluck me out—me who was going to ruin—by means of marriage; rather were they concerned only that I should learn how to make a good speech and persuade people by speaking." Monica apparently believed that an early marriage would get in the way of her son's ambitions—or rather, in the ways of his parent's ambitions for him. In all fairness, Augustine ascribes this motivation fully only to his father— "who basically had no thought for You." His mother, he claims, also thought that his mastery of language arts would contribute not only toward his secular career but also to his eventual turning toward God. She was right on that score, but the paths that brought Augustine to God would be more crooked than even she had imagined.

The story of a theft of forbidden fruit is undoubtedly the most famous single incident in the entirety of the *Confessions.* Augustine and his roving friends robbed a neighbor's pear tree one night, although unmotivated by any need for food. This youthful crime became the occasion for his profound meditation on the nature of sin. The theft was a wholly gratuitous action, one not excused or made comprehensible by some powerful and undeniable survival need. (The great medieval theologian Thomas Aquinas did not regard stealing food as a sin, when it was a matter of survival.) Because the motivation was not some obvious good (and all ancient philosophers agreed that human actions aimed at some perceived good), a riddle presents itself. In this riddle is concealed a secret of the human relation to God, a secret that reveals itself only when that relation has been lost or damaged. For the sake of unraveling this riddle, Augustine relates the episode of the pear tree.

Augustine argues that a natural sense of right and wrong is present within us, even apart from God's revealed law. But, as John Calvin would later emphasize in his own theological system, this knowledge can never be the basis for salvation. The presence of this natural conscience is evident in the actions of criminals. Thieves do not allow other thieves to steal from them, even if one thief is rich and the other steals from him motivated solely by necessity. This amounts to a tacit recognition on the part of those who commit this evil that it is an obvious evil, insofar as they would experience it that way themselves if it were done to them. In regard to his adolescent crime, Augustine admits he knew that it was wrong, and that it was this very wrong that he longed to do. "I wanted to commit theft and did it, though compelled by no neediness apart from a poverty of justice and a contempt for it, and from a bloatedness with iniquity. For I stole what I had plenty and better of." Neither he nor his partners in crime took much joy in the pears they shook down from the unwitting neighbor's tree. They had a taste and threw the rest to the pigs. So why did he do it? "What was my heart seeking there, that I would be wicked for nothing, that there would be no ground for my wickedness? It was filthy and I loved it." How difficult it is to look back on past actions we now regret and admit to ourselves that our joy was somehow mostly in the transgression itself! Because Augustine saw truly into his motivation for this relatively minor crime, he was able to plumb the depths of evil. Not all transgressions reveal the structure of sin so clearly. But still, it is all too easy, even in our moments of critical recollection, to come up with some supposed good we sought in actions we now believe to have been altogether wrong.

Augustine's line of questioning in his ruminations upon the pear tree episode departs from what would have been the usual procedure followed by judicial inquiries of his day. Prosecutors knew they must establish a credible motive, or—as Augustine says—establish that there was either "a desire to obtain some one of those goods that we call lower or a fear of losing something." Augustine, following the tradition of ancient philosophy, distinguished between goods one could lose through accident, folly, or the actions of another and goods such as justice or beatitude that were not subject to accidental loss. The desire for such lower goods is behind a great deal of human action. Is it possible that one would murder without reason? Or commit savage acts of cruelty? No, even in regard to the notorious Catiline (a conspirator whom Cicero famously led Rome to take action against), who was said to be cruel for cruelty's own sake, a motive could be found: "lest through inactivity the hand or mind should become slack." Augustine writes that "not even Catiline himself loved his crimes but there was certainly something else for the sake of which he did them."

> What did I, an unhappy person, love in you, O my theft, O you my nocturnal crime of my sixteenth year of age? For you were not lovely, since you were theft. But are you indeed anything that I should address you? Those pears that we stole were lovely, as they were Your creation, O loveliest of all, Creator of all,

good God, God the highest Good and my true good. Those pears were lovely, but they were not what my unhappy soul longed for. An abundance of better ones was available for me. But I picked them only to steal them. For I cast our pickings away, having feasted only on the wickedness there, which I rejoiced to enjoy. If anything of those pears entered my mouth, its savor was the crime. Now, O Lord my God, I am seeking what in the theft delighted me: lo and behold, there is no beauty in it. I'm not talking about the attractiveness one finds in equality and wisdom, nor even the sort one finds in the human mind, memory, senses, or growing life. Nor was it attractive like the stars which adorn their stations, like the earth or sea full of their progeny, which by giving birth replace those passing away; nor was there even the deficient and shadowy beauty one finds in deceptive vices. (*Conf.* II, 12)

What, then, of his motive for sinning as a youth in this way? What, then, of the motive behind all sins, particularly those that are traits of character as opposed to merely single actions, as was the case for Augustine's teenage larceny? Turning to a discussion of what is usually translated "vices" ("weaknesses of character" better catches the sense), Augustine compiles a list of the "deceptive vices"—habits of mind encompassing everything from haughtiness to laziness. All of them are misguided imitations of God. Haughtiness, or pride (a word that in Augustine's Latin has a strong negative ring) imitates God's lofty remove—but God alone is far removed from sin. What he means by pride should not be confused with what we would call self-esteem. Theologically speaking, pride is a weakness in being a defect on the part of the creature that pertains to its perception of self. For pride means an arrogation on the creature's part of something that properly belongs to God alone.

A similar thing can be observed in the case of ambition, something Augustine had come to see as a weakness in himself. Ambition involves seeking glory and honor, but God alone is to be given honor and glory. God's glory is eternal and thus not dependent, as human honor is, upon the opinion of faulty and fickle human beings. Augustine's analysis of cruelty is much the same as the theory maintained a thousand years later by Machiavelli. Cruelty is employed by people in power to make themselves feared and thus maintain their power. The well-known instances of police brutality are generally cases where the level of violence seems designed to "teach a lesson" so that none dare resist the authority of the police and ultimately of the state and its laws. Yet God alone, Augustine says, is truly to be feared. Any attempt by human beings to make themselves feared amounts to setting up themselves in the place of God. And this is clearly sin.

The same dynamic applies to something most of us would probably like a little more of: luxury. People who cultivate luxury, along the lines of Augustine's analysis, don't want it called luxury, because that sounds like a vice. We prefer to regard it as a fullness and an abundance, and are perhaps appropriately thankful for it. But to have all things in moderation is not enough for the true cultivators of luxury. This mode of behavior, Augustine maintains, is a sinful and futile attempt to attain the life of God, who alone is "Fullness and an unfailing Plenitude of incorruptible sweetness." Those who attempt to get goods that are not their own miss the mark. In fact, they fail to realize the goods that could belong to them, if only they would maintain a right relation to the source of all. Augustine puts it in the graphic language he borrows from the biblical prophets: "the soul commits fornication when it turns from You and seeks things that are pure and unstained outside of You. It does not find them unless it should return to You." It's all about acknowledging ourselves as creaturely beings who are dependent upon the Great Good for all our goods.

How does this analysis relate to the pear-tree incident? It has to do with Augustine's notion that many typical modes of sins are misbegotten imitations of aspects of God. "All who set themselves far from You and raise themselves up against You, imitate You in a twisted manner. But even in their imitating You in this fashion they give a sign that You are the creator of every nature and that accordingly there exists nowhere that they could in any way escape from You." How, then, was Augustine's act of theft a twisted imitation of the creator? Recall how he acknowledged that theft not only is against God's law but also violates natural law, the law that remains present even in the deficient conscience of thieves. Augustine's delight in doing what was not permitted simply because it was not permitted was an illusory joy of attaining a freedom that in reality wasn't his. Drawing on an image from the apostle Paul, Augustine depicts himself as a captive of the law, someone unable to extricate himself from a nature to which law is necessarily present. In this sense he was a prisoner who sought to act the part of a free person. He could succeed in achieving only what he calls a "handcuffed freedom." Absolute freedom does not exist for human beings. We create neither ourselves nor the contexts and possibilities of our actions. He was "doing with impunity what was not permitted for the sake of a shadowy likeness of omnipotence." To act as though one has no limits is nothing other than to play at being God.

Augustine's analysis, however, does not stop here. He knows well that his actions cannot be regarded just as one individual's sinning for his own individual reasons. There was a social context to his sin; and this social context should not be construed as a purely neutral jelly surrounding the meat of the matter. He needed companionship, a band of fugitives to share his fugitive delight. They were his fellows in crime, and his fellows in laughter at those who futilely railed at the unknown culprits and their undetected crime.

> Alone I would not have committed that theft, where what pleased me was not what I was stealing but the fact that I was stealing. Doing this alone would not have pleased me so well, nor would I have done it. O friendship so clearly unfriendly, untraceable seducer of the mind! It was a craving to do harm as a sport and a joke, an appetite to wrong another person, apart from any desire for revenge or for my own gain. It was just that someone said "Come on, let's do it"—and one is ashamed not to be shameless. (*Conf.* II, 17)

From the theologians of the early church through the scholastics of the Middle Ages, from the Protestant Reformers to modern Christian thinkers, Christian theologians have always been conscious of the collective dimension of sin. Without losing sight of the responsibility of the individual, Augustine too insists on the social context of sin. The New Testament phrase "the kingdom of this world" had for Augustine a very concrete reality in the Roman Empire, Christian though it had become by his day. A full consideration of human history and the role of human communities in sin will be a topic he explores in one of the great and expansive works of his later career, *The City of God*.

CHAPTER THREE

A Young Man on His Own

Things really got hot when Augustine was sent to study rhetoric in Carthage, the capital and cultural center of Roman Africa. His family had obtained financial help from the local patrician Romanianus to send their promising seventeen-year-old to Carthage to complete his education in style. But they had no idea all the elements of style with which their son was going to spice up his college life!

I came to Carthage, and a crackling frying pan of illicit loves surrounded me. I wasn't in love yet, but I was in love with love, and from a deeply hidden longing I hated myself for longing less. I was looking for something to love, loving to love, and I hated the idea of a carefree existence and a life without hidden traps. This was because there was a famine inside me for interior food, for You Yourself, my God. I wasn't starving from that famine; to the contrary, I was without any desire for incorruptible food. Not that I'd had my fill of it; rather, the emptier I was the more fastidious I became. And that was why my soul was not doing well: covered in sores it thrust itself outward, miserably eager to be scratched by contact with things of the senses. But had they not a hold on my soul, they certainly would not have been loved. To love and be loved was sweet to me, especially if I could enjoy the body of the one who loved me. So I contaminated the vein of friendship with the squalor of eager desire, I fogged up its brightness with the deep pit of lust. And although I was filthy and disreputable, I presented myself as refined and cosmopolitan out of an overflowing sense of vanity. I stumbled in love as well, by which I had been trying to be captured. My God, my Compassion, how much bitterness You sprinkled into that sweetness, how good You were! For I was loved, I attained the shackle of enjoying love and was happily tied up with woeful bindings. The result was that I was beaten by burning iron rods of jealousy, suspicions, fears, rages, and quarrels. (*Conf.* III, 1)

Augustine does not tell us the details of his love affair. We know that he soon settled down with one girl—the one he'd met in Carthage and brought home after the school term. Augustine hooked up with this woman when he was sixteen, and he lived faithfully with her for more than a dozen years. The relationship came to his end when it became an obstacle to his socially-motivated and arranged marriage. Propriety demanded sending her back to Africa.

Augustine never tells us the woman's name. Some people may have difficulty forgiving him for what seems to be an abysmal piece of impersonality and distancing. The most likely reason he concealed her name was to protect her from unwanted and prurient attention. He tells us later that she went back to Africa, vowing never to take another man. She may well have entered a convent of sorts. In that time, their "living together," and even having a child together, was not considered particularly immoral. She would have been considered his common-law wife. The real issue was social, not moral. She came from a lower social class than Augustine, which meant that any children they had would take her status, not his. Thus she didn't fit the bill for the kind of wife Augustine—and his mother—were looking for.

Augustine's discussion of his passion for love brings him to analyze his other passions. He loved the theater, especially the plays that depicted people in love along with all of love's attendant miseries. Augustine was struck by the link between passion and compassion. The reason is more evident when we look at the Latin, starting with a word we recognize: misery. The Latin abstract noun from which this comes—*miseria*—means the same as the English, unhappiness or wretchedness. But English doesn't have an adjective built on the same stem that shows the same basic meaning. Latin *miser* means an unhappy or pitiable person, which is not the sense of our word "miser." These words come from the Latin verb *misereor*, which means to take pity or have compassion upon someone. This meaning is well caught by the English "commiserate." But English can't reach the Latin word *misericordia*, which we translate as "pity" or "compassion." (The literal translation "having a heart tuned to another's unhappiness" is clearly too long winded!) Throughout the Bible, God is depicted as compassionate, obviously an important aspect of God's nature. It may well be a universal human experience that goodness and mercy are intimately linked.

What gets Augustine going on the subject of his love for plays is the paradox that he, like other theater-goers, positively enjoyed scenes of peoples' miseries. In fact, he went to the theater precisely in order to partake of the feelings of sorrow and woe that come from sympathizing with the feelings of others. Why, Augustine asks, would you want to suffer vicariously the sufferings of others on stage, when you would be loathe to suffer them in reality?

> Shows on stage grabbed me, being filled with images of my own miseries and sparks for my fire. But why is it that in a theater people want to grieve when they

watch sad and tragic scenes which they themselves would not want to suffer? Yet spectators want to suffer grief from them—the grief itself is the pleasure. What is this but miserable insanity? For the more someone is moved by these spectacles, the less sane the person is in regard to these emotions—although one normally calls it misery when one suffers them oneself, but compassion to suffer them when it has to do with other people. But really, what kind of compassion can there be when it comes to these fictitious and theatrical scenes? The audience is not drawn in to help those suffering, but is merely invited to grieve. More favor is bestowed upon the author of these representations, when the audience sorrows more deeply. If the misfortunes—be they ancient history or mythic—of the people are presented so that the spectators feel no grief, they leave carping and criticizing. But if they do grieve, they remain rapt and rejoicing. So tears and grief are loved! No doubt everyone wants to rejoice. Is grief loved for this reason: that although it pleases no-one to be miserable, but being compassionate is pleasing—and this can't happen without grieving? This too arises from that vein of friendship. But where does it go? Where does it flow? To run down into that torrent of bubbling tar, into giant waves of hellish lusts? The vein of friendship is itself transformed into these waves and whirled around by its own initiative, rendering it torn off and thrown down from its celestial calm. So is compassion to be repudiated? No way—then let grief be loved sometimes. Just be on guard against uncleanliness. . . .

I'm not saying I am uncompassionate now. Back then I rejoiced in lovers on stage, as they enjoyed themselves in their transgressions. Despite the fact that the things performed were imaginary, when the characters lost each other, I partook in a way of their sadness. At any rate, both the rejoicing and the sadness delighted me. Now, however, I have more compassion for those rejoicing in their transgressions than for those who have suffered supposed difficulties due to an obstacle to their pernicious pleasure and the loss of their miserable happiness. This compassion I have now is surely truer, but it is a compassion in which grief gives no delight. . . . But back then I loved to grieve, unhappy as I was, and I was seeking something to grieve about. When it came to the grief of others, which were fictional and staged, an actor's performance pleased me better and drew me in more strongly to the degree that my tears were wrested out. Is it any wonder that as an unhappy sheep wandering away from Your flock, impatient of Your custody, I would get fouled by a disgusting mange? And that was the source of my love for grief. It wasn't for grief that hit deeper home—I did not love to undergo the kinds of things I watched—rather it was a love for fictional performances, by which I was scratched on the surface. But the scratching, as it were, of those fingernails was followed by a hot swelling, a putrification, and an awful bloody mess. Such a life as mine couldn't really be called life, could it, O my God? (*Conf.* III, 2–4)

The relationship between opposites—life and death, pleasure and pain—exercised the mind of ancient philosophers, especially Plato in his Socratic dialogues. In the dialogue describing Socrates' final moments before execution, the manacles on his ankles are removed so he can better enjoy the visit of his friends. With his usual irony, the philosopher remarks on the pleasure afforded by the loosening of the leg-irons. He notes the odd connection of pleasure and pain, how they always seem to follow closely upon each another. Augustine's analysis of pleasures and pains in a stage drama provides a strange twist on the old philosophical conundrum. In talking of his youthful love of the theater, he begins with an admission of his unhappiness at that time. He goes on to assume from this, without demonstration, that the more one suffers emotional disorders within, the more one will be inclined to enjoy the depiction of such disorders without. More distressing to Augustine is the fact that whatever compassion the theater evoked, it did not serve compassion's usual function: to move one person to help another. Thus this feeling, and its true function, is denatured when elicited by the fictions of the theater.

At the time, such considerations did not disturb his enjoyment. Augustine loved being brought to tears by a fine performance; his criticism was confined to the quality of the dramatic production. He was a student of fine poetry and great prose: The ability to appreciate and reproduce these was the purpose of his education. No doubt his frequenting the theater was one of those ways of putting on airs and fancying himself a fine fellow, as he puts it at the opening of book III. At that time in Carthage, he lived with a rowdy bunch of students known as the Overturners. Augustine denies ever taking part in their "overturnings," which seem to have consisted largely of intimidating freshmen with cruelty and cynicism. He claims that even then he was shocked and repelled by their behavior. But however much their doings made his moral craw stick in his throat, he lived with them anyway, albeit "with a shameful shamelessness, since I was not like such people." Looking back on them, he judges them more harshly still. Because they took such malevolent joy in breaking the innocence of their juniors, Augustine likens their behavior to that of demons: "What could they be more truly called than Overturners? They themselves had earlier obviously been overturned and twisted by seductive and deceitful hidden spirits, who now mock them in their very love for deceiving and mocking others."

But what was a good boy like Augustine doing with those hoods? He neither approved of their doings nor felt comfortable criticizing them. So why did the smart kid hang out with bad company? Augustine's sense of himself, as retrospectively presented, was that he was cool. He had status, in school, for his intelligence; but he also wanted to be a man about town, not a timid nerd. He seems to have succeeded. By seventeen, he had a regular girlfriend. He was a Latin lover, with a streak of boldness. He relates one scenario to us rather briefly, lest we enjoy too much his tale of lust: "During a celebration of Your holy mass, within the walls of Your church I dared even to conceive a lust and to carry out the business of procuring the fruit of death." Some scholars have imagined him actually having sex within the church. More likely, he spotted an attractive woman there, whom he then connived to meet. It's possible that he could be referring here to his common-law wife: how he met her in church, made arrangements with her family, and proceeded to live with her—sinning, as he later saw it, in his addiction to sex. This addiction was the chief obstacle to being in accord with his deepest spiritual convictions.

Given, then, this steamy environment, this frying pan of lusts all around him, we might be surprised to find out that Augustine experienced his first conversion in these years in Carthage. By "conversion," I mean merely one of those turning points he flags in the *Confessions*. Oddly enough, what triggered this first (incomplete) conversion was a book of pagan philosophy. His reading of this book swept him off the career track that would have turned him into a lawyer and repaid his parents' worldly expenditures.

Following the usual curriculum of the time I came across a book of some Cicero fellow. Practically everyone admires his tongue—though not his heart. But that book of his contains an exhortation to philosophy and is called *Hortensius*. That book definitely altered my state of mind. It even altered my prayers toward You Yourself, O Lord, making me have different hopes and desires. Suddenly every empty hope seemed to me not worthwhile. With an intense burning in my heart, I conceived a lust for the immortality of wisdom. I had begun to rise up to return to You. . . . How I was on fire, O my God, how I was on fire to spin away from earthly things to You—and I had no idea what You were doing with me. For wisdom is present with You. Now, love of wisdom has a name in Greek, philosophy, under which name that text had reached me. . . . But You

know, O Light of my heart, that since the apostolic
writings were as yet unknown to me, just one thing
in that exhortation delighted me: that it would not
have me love this or that sect but wisdom itself,
whatever it was, and that I would love, seek, follow,
hold, and embrace it heartily. I was stirred up by that
text, inflamed, set on fire. Just one thing held me
back from a total combustion: that the name of
Christ was not there. For this name of my Savior
Your Son, O Lord, this name had my tender heart
dutifully drunk in along with my mother's milk and
it was holding it deep within. Whatsoever was without this name, however well-written, proper, and
true, did not altogether grab me. And so I set my
mind to look into the holy Scriptures and to see what
sort of writings they were. (*Conf.* III, 7–8)

A pagan work, then, one that presented wisdom itself as
the goal of philosophy rather than a particular philosophical school, set Augustine to reading the Bible! We might
expect that a boy brought up by such a Christian mother
would have read the Bible at home. But early Christians
did not have Bibles at home; this is something we owe to
the invention of the printing press and the Protestant
Reformation. In Augustine's world, most people couldn't
read. Home Bibles would have been far too expensive for
any but the very wealthy to own. Certain passages of Scripture were learned by those preparing for baptism, but
Augustine hadn't gotten that far. It's not that Christianity
wasn't in some sense a "religion of the book" back then,
but it was so in a rather different way. The Bible was read
at worship services (in longer passages than today); and
churches made it available for those who had the skills and
the inclination to study it. As a learned young man, Augustine was in possession of these prerequisites, but his first

forays into Scripture met with no success. The reason why may strike us as peculiar, for it had to do with literary style.

Modern readers may be puzzled by the fact that the style in which the Bible was written could prevent an intelligent reader from grasping the content's moral and religious depth. How could Augustine be so shallow? Readers of English Bibles do not, however, face the situation Augustine confronted when he opened the Latin Bible of his day. We are familiar with the Authorized, or King James, Version, which is a monument of superb English prose. The loftiness of the subject is matched by the dignity of the diction. The most recent revision of the King James Bible— the New Revised Standard Version—also consists of elegant prose and poetry in vivid contemporary English. A number of other contemporary translations, however, have aimed to produce versions that can be understood by people who possess only the most rudimentary literacy. Imagine if you were a professor of English literature, accustomed to reading Shakespeare and Milton, and the only Bible you could find was that kind of simplified translation. You might read further on the grounds that style and content can be independent of each other—but this belief would have contradicted the presuppositions of Augustine and the literary culture of his day. All his training in literature and rhetoric would have led him to believe that style and content were closely related. A great matter would demand a grand style. For that reason, the mature Augustine notes that the Scriptures are "not accessible to proud minds." Having been one such proud mind in his youth, Augustine was put off by the Bible he read in the clunky and literal Old Latin translation then available. Compared to the exalted character of Cicero's writing, where a great matter was appropriately expressed in a great style, it seemed unworthy of further attention. But looking back, he recognizes that the problem was not in the Scripture but in himself: "my swelling fled before its style, and my sharp mind couldn't penetrate its innards. Nonetheless they were the Scriptures, a sort of writing which grows along with little ones; but I found it demeaning to be a little one. Swollen with arrogance I saw myself as a big man."

Augustine details these events in book III of the *Confessions*: his love of love, his love of theater, his association with the Overturners, his incomplete conversion to philosophy, and his disappointing encounter with the Bible. They all ominously portend the major error of his young adulthood—and it had nothing to do with sex. His sins in that thorny realm entangled only himself and his family; but his involvement with the heretical sect of the Manichees was an error that made his supple mind a purveyor of a far more dangerous contagion.

Manicheism, a gnostic religion founded in the third century, made a considerable impact on the late Roman Empire. Mani, the sect's founder, was born in 216 and had grown up in a Jewish-Christian community in the region of the Tigris river. When he was twenty-four, a revelation from God assured Mani that he was the twin of the Holy Spirit, a second apostle Paul come to bring the latest revision of the good news. Like the apostle Paul, his missionary activities got him in trouble. Mani ended his days in chains (his "passion," as his followers put it), imprisoned by the Persian king, who was not about to tolerate a rival to the official Zoroastrian religion. Manicheism itself, beginning as a Christian heresy, developed into an independent gnostic religion that moved eastward along the silk roads into China, where its last representatives seemed to have died out in the seventeenth century.

Augustine's self-portrait in the *Confessions,* up to the point of his involvement with the Manichees, presents a mixed picture. On the one hand, we see a passionate young man with strong loves and a great capacity for the full range of human feelings. This had made him vulnerable, both to spectacles on stage and to the real-life dramas of love. On the other hand, Augustine worried about the destructive spirit of some of his friends who lived too close to the dark side. However he may have differed from them in possessing a moral sensibility, his association with them indicates that they nonetheless shared something in common. Augustine's conversion to philosophy shows us that he was an idealistic young man, whose sense of the worth of human existence remained untouched by the cynicism and careerism of those around him. His abortive attempt to read the Bible clearly points to a struggle to retain some continuity with the religion of his mother. We should see

him as he portrays himself: a seeker of truth liable to error due to his own impressionable, if insufficiently critical, openness to the way to wisdom.

And so I fell in among men who were egotistically raving. Much given to talk, they were really unspiritual; and their mouths were traps of the devil, a glue composed of a mixture of the syllables of Your Name, of the Lord Jesus Christ, and of the Paraclete our Comforter, the Holy Spirit. These names were never absent from their mouths, but only so far as the sound and the clacking of the tongue went. In other ways their hearts were void of truth. But they were saying "truth, truth," speaking a lot about truth with me—and it never was in them. Rather were they speaking falsities, not only about You who are truly the Truth, but also about the very elements of the world, Your creation. Even when philosophers spoke true things about these elements, I was obliged to pass them by in view of Your love, my Father most high and good, Beauty of all beauties. O Truth, Truth, how intimately even the inner folds of my mind panted after You! It didn't matter that those men who often and in many ways sounded You out to me did so only with the voice, and by their many huge books! These sounds were the dishes which served up the sun and the moon, Your beautiful works, to me as I hungered for You. But these were, in the final analysis, Your works, not You, and they weren't Your first works. For Your prior works were spiritual realities, prior to these physical ones, however bright and heavenly though they be. But I was hungering and thirsting not for those prior works but for You Yourself, O Truth, where there is neither variableness nor shadow of turning. And shimmering apparitions were set before me in those dishes. It had been better to love the sun, true at least to these eyes, than those things which are false and deceive the mind through the eyes. Nonetheless, because I thought they were You, I fell to eating, not indeed with gusto, since those things did not have the taste in my mouth of what You are—nor indeed were You these empty figments. These things didn't nourish me, and I grew emptier still. (*Conf.* III, 10)

When Augustine says that the Manichees served him up the sun and the moon, setting them out in dishes with the names of Christ and the Holy Spirit, he is referring to the prominent role of the heavenly bodies in Manichean cosmology. Mani had taught that the sun, the moon, and the stars were not lifeless physical bodies: They were animated beings, possessing souls. This idea was common among various religions and philosophies of the ancient world. The Manichees put a special twist on it, maintaining that this universe as we now know it is the result of a cosmic struggle between the forces of Good and Evil. This implies something more than the Christian understanding that we are part of a struggle between God and the devil. Unlike Jews, Christians, and Platonist philosophers, who believed that God created the world deliberately with a good end in view, Mani came up with a distinct innovation. The forces of Good and Evil existed, he maintained, from the beginning (a view similar to that of the Persian religion, Zoroastrianism). The universe as we see it now is the result of a battle between these two primal forces. In this battle, the "Good Light," unable to defeat the invading "Evil Darkness," sacrificed a part of itself for the sake of an eventual, future victory over darkness. This self-sacrifice consisted of allowing particles of the light-world to be swallowed up and imprisoned within the forces of darkness. Human beings have particles of light in them, albeit surrounded and plagued by a thick shell of matter. Matter itself is the source of many horrible feelings and cravings that torment the soul. The sun and the moon—part of the light world, or angels, so to speak—are chained in their orbits. Redemption from this prison camp of a world comes through Christ. As the representative par excellence of the light world, Christ descends from the Father of Light to bring a saving knowledge to that remnant of humanity in which the light is still manifest. The Manicheans held that some aspects of Christ's teaching were embedded in the Gospels of the New Testament, but that many passages had been falsified by his followers. However, they held the apostle Paul in high respect and often referred to his letters. The writings of Mani himself were authoritative in this fast-growing albeit unlawful sect. Pagan Roman emperors had declared it illegal, because they associated it with the dangerous Persian empire on their eastern borders. The Christian emperors did not alter the status of this unorthodox group, because the bishops who advised them were also eager for its suppression.

But what could have attracted Augustine to the Manichees and their elaborate mythology? He tells us that it was their posture as philosophical Christians searching for the truth, asking questions, and not taking things on authority. Certainly their teaching differed sharply from the universal (or "catholic") and apostolic Church. Mani's special revelation made his followers take a critical view of the Old Testament. Much of this had already been fodder for other gnostic groups. To these critics, the Creator God of the Old Testament appeared to be harsh, arbitrary, and vengeful, a far cry from the Father of Mercy announced by Jesus Christ, who was not of this world. Through their moralistic objections to biblical descriptions of the Creator, the Manichees set themselves up as critical minds, critical of authorities who told you "just believe," and critical of writings whose truth and consistency were not self-evident. The young intellectual Augustine found their approach refreshing, at least initially. Because the name of Christ and the Holy Spirit were always on their lips, he supposed them to be in more perfect possession of the Christian truth than those simple believers in the church who accepted literally and uncritically the stories about God in the Scriptures.

> I was ignorant of that other Being, which really exists. I was goaded, as it were, into favoring those stupid deceivers when they posed questions to me. "Where does evil come from?" "Is God bound by a corporeal form?" "Does God have hair and fingernails?" "Can we consider men just who had many wives all at once? Can we consider men just who have offered animal sacrifices, or have killed people?" Ignorant of these matters, I was shaken up. Although I was departing from the truth, to myself I seemed to be headed toward it. This was because I had not understood that evil exists only as a privation: a subtraction of a

good from something to the point where it ceases to exist at all. How was I to have seen this, being someone whose eyesight went no further than a body and whose mind saw no further than a phantom? I had not come to understand that God was Spirit, the sort to Whom belonged no members of length, breadth, or mass. Any mass is less in one part than in its whole. If it is an infinite mass, some part of it, defined by a certain space, is less than the whole infinity. A mass does not contain itself complete all over, as Spirit does, as God does. I was utterly ignorant about what it was in us that made us exist, utterly ignorant why we are said in Scripture to be made "in the the image of God" [Gen. 1:27]. (*Conf.* III, 12)

This lack of theological understanding about God was the problem. The Manichees may indeed have believed themselves to possess the Christian truth, but for Augustine this was not a way he could have gotten to God at all. Later he came to the understanding that there is only one true Christianity: the one propounded by the church that is one, universal, and founded by the apostles. He sees his time among the Manichees as lived not in a real relation to God the Creator. Rather he was addicted to an unwholesome substitute: fantastic myths and stories they told about God and the drama of redemption. The dishes of a false theology, even though served up under true names, could not satisfy that innate human hunger for God. The goodies of the Manichean cosmology were not only dissimilar to God, as would be any physical bodies or representations of bodies, they were even more unreal. He calls them "apparitions" of physical things, because they were just ideas of things that don't exist. Our images of physical things, which at least really exist, are more certain than representations of beings whose existence we merely infer. The long and short of it is that while he was in the Manichees, Augustine was separated from God by several levels of reality. Not only did he not have an adequate image or representation of God, but he substituted in its place ideas which themselves either were false or referred only to fictional entities. Ironically, Augustine's separation from the Manichees came not through Christianity, but through a deeper knowledge of the true workings of the heavenly bodies as understood by ancient astronomers.

We may well wonder what Augustine's pious mother Monica thought of all this Manichean mishmash. Upon completing his schooling in Carthage, he returned to Thagaste with a girlfriend, a baby, and a set of shocking beliefs. For a while his mother refused to let him live at home. She relented from this policy only when God granted her a dream reassuring her that she would not forever lose her son to hell. That, of course, was her great fear—not unlike that of many a pious parent today whose children are imprinted with elements of the world that

seem so contradictory to Christian truth. Augustine paints a poignant picture of how his mother cried out to God in her distress, and how she was answered.

> From on high You sent Your hand and tore my soul out of that deep darkness, when my mother, Your faithful woman, wept about me to You. She wept more than mothers do over the bodies of their dead children. She looked upon my death from the perspective of her faith and from the spirit she had from You; and You heard her, O Lord. You heard, and You did not despise her tears as they flowed forth and watered the ground under her eyes everywhere she prayed. You heard her. For where else did that dream come from? . . . For she saw herself standing on a certain wooden ruler, and there came to her a shining and happy youth, smiling at her as she was mourning and consumed with sorrow. The youth, after he had inquired of her the reasons for her sorrowfulness and daily tears, . . . directed and admonished her, that she might be at ease, to observe and see that where she was, there too I would be. Observing what was where, she saw me standing next to her on the same ruler. . . . Where too did that come from, that when she had told me about the vision itself and I was trying to detract from it by saying that she should not despair about herself coming to be where I was, that she immediately without any hesitation said, "no, it wasn't said to me where he is, there you too will be, but where you are there he too will be."? (*Conf.* III, 19–20)

Augustine tells us that his mother's quick response to his comment moved him more than the dream itself. Her response showed confidence in God, a confidence repaid after a space of another nine years. Monica's sense that God was on the case the whole time did not cause her either to cease her tearful prayers or to cease looking for ways to bring her wayward son back around. Augustine recounts how his mother approached a bishop, whose intellect could perhaps have persuaded her son. The bishop she visited was in fact an excellent choice for the task. His own mother had entrusted his upbringing to the Manichees. Thus he had become deeply acquainted with all the Manichean writings but, upon growing older, had realized their unsoundness. He then quit the sect and joined the Catholic Church. This bishop, wise in the ways of human nature, advised Monica to leave Augustine alone to discover for himself the errors, both of the Manichees and himself. Monica kept badgering the bishop to intervene. He eventually got annoyed and sent her away with an assurance: "It is not possible that the son of such tears would perish." Those words, Augustine tells us, she repeated to him again and again as if they had fallen from heaven.

CHAPTER FOUR

A Professional Teacher

Augustine had returned home only to be kicked out by his mother for his Manichean beliefs—not for his girlfriend. But we should not think of him as a slacker, who came back from college and lived at home with nothing to do but have a good time. Thanks to his patron, Augustine was professionally launched. Romanianus, the local grandee who had provided liberally for Augustine's education, now gave him a home during his mother's disfavor. With his training and this patronage, Augustine had prospects for mobility. He quickly obtained a position in Carthage, when a tragic event mandated a move.

These were Augustine's Manichean years, from the age of nineteen to twenty-eight. "We were being seduced and were seducing, deceived and deceiving in a variety of lusts: outwardly through teaching of the liberal arts, in secret under the deceptive name of religion. Arrogant in the one and superstitious in the other, we were everywhere devoid of substance." From the outside, Augustine's rather successful life—career, friends, family, a religious community—appears quite normal. He takes some care to let his readers know that he was, despite his various failings, a pretty good guy. He admits that as a professor of rhetoric, he liked to have "what are called good students, whom I was without any deception teaching to be deceptive—not for them to plead in court to take the life of a person, but sometimes to plead for the life of a guilty one." We learn also of Augustine's scruples in a competition for which he had submitted some poetry for a play. Many people in his position would have sought to influence the judges in some way—including occult means. An acquaintance was eager to do the job, by sacrificing an animal to make the spirits favorable. Augustine refused this offer, perhaps in part due to the animal rights sensitivity cultivated by Manichees, whose Elect were strictly vegetarian. And what about the mother of his son Adeodatus (whose name means "given by God")? Augustine tells us that the arrangement was decent, even virtuous in some respects, despite the fact that it was not a true marriage nor motivated by appropriate ends.

> I had a woman in those years. Not acknowledged by what is called legitimate marriage, she was a woman whom my roving heat, totally lacking judgment, had tracked down. But she was my one woman, and I even maintained sexual fidelity to her. This, evi-

dently, was a way for me to experience by example what a difference there is between the measured manner of marriage—a covenant undertaken for the sake of procreation—and a contract of lustful love, where a child is born even against one's wishes. But once born, children compel you to love them. (*Conf.* IV, 2)

Augustine's self-presentation during this period focuses not on his teaching or his family life but rather on the way in which the spiritual substance of his life—his religious wanderings, his personal difficulties, and his intellectual errors—seemed somewhat off kilter. He relates how he got involved with astrology. He learned the "science" of it (how to cast horoscopes), not in order to make money (that his teaching earned him) but because he was deceived by it. Not even the wise advice of an old physician, an ex-astrologer himself, could dissuade him from this deception. Nor could the urgings of his dear friend Nebridius, "who laughed at that entire species of divination," turn him against it. The authority of the authors of those astrological tomes seemed weightier to him. Also, no one had been able to explain away the realized predictions of astrologers. Astrology was much in vogue in the ancient world, as it is today in many cultures. Those who cultivate those arts are often honored by others who are impressed with the claims of this "science." Only later, when Augustine found clear disproof of astrology, did he realize that this too was one of the several ways in which while deceiving others, he was himself deceived.

The most distressing event of Augustine's early life was the death of a friend. He had known this young man since grade school, although they had become close friends only after Augustine's return to Thagaste. Augustine segues the story of the friend's death into a discussion of friendship and our tendency to love mortal things in themselves rather than in God. This topic is a reprise of the love and grief theme developed earlier. The very loves that life in the flesh engenders, born of the beauties of the created order, are destined to bring sorrow in their wake. For that which constitutes the very essence of love—its rhythm of longing and fulfillment—also opens the possibility of loss when what is loved is finite. The self in its fullness, a creature made according to the image of God, bears as it were a trace of the divine infinity in its infinity of desire. But because the objects of our desire are finite, our loves end up being a desperate clawing after things that do not keep. The mature Augustine found a solution. True friendship must be cemented by God among "those who stick together by the love spread in our hearts by the Holy Spirit which has been given to us" (see Rom. 5:5, a favorite verse of his). What he had with his friend who died, sweet

though it was to him, could not have been true friendship, for they were mutually implicated in religious error and were outside that friendship of Spirit-inspired love.

I turned him away from the true faith (which he held as a child neither deeply nor completely) and toward those superstitious and pernicious fables, because of which my mother was weeping over me. With me he was now going astray in his mind; and my soul could not be without him. But lo and behold, You were at the backs of Your runaways, O God, a fountain of both mercies and revenge, You who convert us to Yourself by marvelous means. Behold, You took the man from this life, when barely a year in our friendship had been completed, sweet though it was to me beyond all the sweetness of that life of mine. . . . What did you do then, my God, and how the abyss of Your judgments defies investigation! For when he was worn down by the fever, he lay comatose for a long time in a deathly sweat; despaired of, he was baptized in a state of unconsciousness. It didn't matter to me, as I presumed that his soul would hold on to what he had received from me, not to what had happened to his body while he was unconscious. But it turned out quite otherwise. For he recovered and became healthy; and at the first chance I had to speak with him (now I was ready as soon as he was able, given that I did not leave his side, we having been very dependent upon each other), I tried to laugh it off with him, as if he were going to laugh with me at that baptism which he had received when he was remote from his mind and consciousness. He had, however, already learned that he had received baptism. Contrary to my expectation, he looked with horror upon me as an enemy, and he admonished me with a surprising and sudden frankness of speech that

> if I wanted to be his friend, I would cease to say such
> things to him. Now I, dumbfounded and upset, with-
> held all my feelings so he could first rest up and fully
> regain his strength of health, at which point I could
> do with him what I wanted. But he was torn out of
> the clutches of my insanity, to be preserved with You
> for my consolation: when I was absent a few days
> later, the fever recurred and he died. (*Conf.* IV, 7–8)

The grief that Augustine experienced over the death of his dear friend crushed him. His heart was darkened by the shadows of sorrow. Wherever he turned his eyes "was death." His home town was torture for him. All those places they had frequented together were now desolating reminders of his friend's absence. The degree of his sorrow made himself inexplicable to himself. "I became to myself one big question." Telling himself to hope in God brought no relief, for the God he imagined was less real than the dear friend he had lost. Instead of love, there were only tears, now his soul's only relief.

Typical of the way Augustine proceeds in the *Confessions*, the story of his friend's death opens onto a larger discussion. How do tears, in themselves a bitter thing, become a source of pleasure? The answer lies not in the incidental nature of the loss, as if it were one cloud sullying an otherwise beauti-ful day. Rather, the wound of the mourning soul, to be cov-ered over only by passing time, discloses something about the state of that soul prior to its dreadful loss. Thus, he writes, "I was an unhappy person; unhappy is the state of all people who have been overcome by the friendship for mor-tal things and are shattered when they lose them, and then come to experience the unhappiness by which they were unhappy even before the loss." Different from the heroes of the stage who prefer to die together than live apart, Augustine experienced the feeling of hating to live and yet fearing death. The death of this close friend seems to have placed everyone he loved under the sentence of death. Even more, he himself felt dead. His head echoed with a verse from the Roman poet Horace, that a friend is "half of one's own soul" (*Odes*, I, 3, 8). It seemed to Augustine a marvel that he could live at all after his other half had died.

"Times are not idle," wrote Augustine, to account for how his mourning faded away. He gradually came to be comforted by his friends, and to embrace the things he always enjoyed: talking, arguing, reading books together, and rejoicing in mutual friendships. Through all the pleasures of human company their "minds and souls were set afire so to make many one" (*ex pluribus unum*, his Latin reads). But as he looks back, Augustine reflects on the problem with loving creatures

while not loving their Creator rightly. The beauty we love in creatures is beauty from God; but God alone is truly beautiful, for God alone truly is. The beauty of all the world's flowers fades. No wonder all loves are tangled in sorrow—though love we must.

> "O God of power, turn us around and show us Your face, and we shall be saved" [Ps. 80:7]. For whatsoever way the human soul turns itself, if it be to anywhere apart from You, it is nailed to sorrows, even if it is nailed to those beautiful things outside You and outside itself. But these beauties would not exist at all unless they were from You. (*Conf.* IV, 15)

During those years in which Augustine regarded himself as "loving lower beauties," his conversations with friends on the topic of beauty led him to compose a book entitled *On the Beautiful and the Fitting*, dedicated to a Roman orator named Hierius. Augustine had never been to Rome and thus had never met this man. But Hierius had a reputation as a great speaker; and Augustine, now professor of rhetoric in Carthage, was quite starstruck with him. His love for this Hierius had been inspired by those who loved him and praised him to Augustine. Looking back, Augustine sees the reason for all that admiration: "I loved him as the type of man I myself would like to be." He interprets the episode as pride, a case of his having been blown around in the wind of public opinion. Nevertheless, he confesses, "I was secretly being guided by You." Even in this careerist move—Augustine admits he hoped his book would come into Hierius's hands—God was somehow present. But the mode of that Presence was not such that Augustine could yet conceive God as Spirit. He was stuck on the notion that all beings, even God, were corporeal. He hadn't an idea for what he would later discover as spiritual reality.

CHAPTER FIVE

Leaving Behind

I remained an unhappy place to myself where I could bear neither to be nor to leave. Where could my heart flee to from itself? Where could I flee to from myself? Where would I not follow myself? I fled my homeland all the same, since my eyes searched for him less in places where they weren't used to seeing him. So I left the town of Thagaste for Carthage. (*Conf.* IV, 12)

A change of place promises a change of mind, so Augustine left his home town. Fleeing his grief, he also fled the tattered reminiscences of the joy he had in his friend. His memory of this joy was now sorrow itself. Carthage was Africa's big city, where Augustine found a teaching position. Unfortunately, the students there were very unruly. He left for Rome, which promised better working conditions, bringing his Manichean beliefs with him. Shortly thereafter he moved to Milan for a better appointment. There Augustine would come in contact with Ambrose the bishop. Inner movement also took place during this year of his life, a year that saw him leave Africa for Italy. When Augustine traveled to Milan, he left his Manichean church behind, although he was not yet convinced of the Catholic one.

> At that time a certain Manichean bishop by the name of Faustus came to Carthage. A death-trap he was for the many people he had entangled in the snare of his sweet speech. Although I too praised it, even then I was aware of the difference between truth—which I was avid to learn—and sweet speech. But it wasn't for the quality of the vessels in which his ideas were served that I looked up to him. It was rather that this Faustus was always mentioned by them for the knowledge he could put out for consumption. The fame of this man had been proclaimed to me: he was very learned in all the established fields, and especially expert in the liberal arts. (*Conf.* V, 3)

Augustine was twenty-nine when the reknowned Manichean teacher Faustus came to Carthage. "Faustus, Faustus, Faustus" had been the refrain from his Manichean friends in response to his probing questions, which none of them could adequately address. Some of these had to do with matters of astronomy. Augustine, though a professor of rhetoric, was liberally educated. He had some knowledge of the natural sciences, including astronomy. This was essential to drawing up horoscopes. But the Manichean books also contained teachings about the heavenly bodies, as many religious movements of the time did. The problem was that these teachings differed from the scientific astronomy Augustine regarded as authoritative in these matters. Astronomers had reliably predicted eclipses, so Augustine assumed that their general picture of the universe was sound. He found it distressing that Mani's picture of the universe was quite different! Augustine's Manichee friends assured him that when Faustus arrived, he would clear everything up.

> When Faustus came, I found him a cultivated man, someone pleasing to listen to. When speaking about the things Manicheans were always talking about, he

chattered on much more sweetly. But how could even
the best waiter minister to my thirst with those pricey
goblets? My ears were already stuffed with such
things. Because things were said better did not make
them seem better to me; because things were well
spoken did not make them true; because a man's face
is appealing and his language commendable does not
make his soul wise. (*Conf.* V, 10)

Faustus, then, was not all he had been cracked up to be.
Even so, Augustine found that they had an interest in
common, a love they could share apart from the error of
their religion: Latin prose. Here Augustine was the professional, and Faustus the gifted if limited amateur. Faustus knew poetry, some Cicero, and a smattering of the
Stoic philosopher Seneca. He was a talented speaker who
practiced assiduously, but so far as learning went, he made
no claims to it—a point Augustine holds to his credit.
How much more foolish was Mani, who dared to construct a whole myth about the universe that contradicted
readily known scientific facts! As a bishop, Augustine
sometimes had to hear fellow Christians airing ideas that
were in direct contradiction to commonly known facts of
the universe. He put up with them patiently enough, as
long as their mistaken opinions did not imply anything
unworthy about God, the Creator. Their errors concerned
only creaturely matters and did not obstruct their having
the necessary knowledge of the faith. But the mistakes in
the Manichean writings about aspects of the creation,
along with Faustus's inability to shed light on the problem, led Augustine to despair of getting a satisfactory
response. "Thus this Faustus who had been a death-trap
for many," he writes, "had begun to loosen the trap in
which I had been caught—though he neither intended
this nor was aware of it." Despite this loosening of his

bonds, Augustine still maintained his personal association with the group. They seemed to have been unaware of the degree of his disaffection.

Nonetheless, Augustine's departure for Rome in search of better students brought no departure from the Manichean circles he had been frequenting. The move to Rome had in fact been facilitated by them. The Manichees maintained the same kind of hospitality among their own group that the earliest Christians had. Augustine became very sick upon his arrival in Rome, so he was lucky to have such friends. The Manichean group, including some of the high level "elect," nursed him back to health, little knowing that the sick man's hold on their faith was destined to fade and never recover. Augustine came to see this sickness as a scourge from God. Prominent among those sins he faced at the brink of death was a recent and terrible deception he carried out against his mother. Monica had joined him in Carthage, refusing to go home without him. Yet he had booked passage on a ship with no intention of taking her along. But how to detach from her? Augustine talked her into spending the night in a chapel dedicated to the great Saint Cyprian of that city, while he was supposedly seeing a friend off on a journey. He set out that night, deserting his mother in Carthage. You can bet the furies were at his back!

> Lo and behold, I am welcomed at Rome by the whip of bodily illness. I was headed for hell, hauling all the evil deeds I had committed against You, against myself, and against many others. There were many weighty sins above and beyond the bond of original sin by which we all die in Adam. For You had not yet forgiven each and every one of them in Christ, nor had he "broken down" [Eph. 2:14] on his cross all my hostile actions I had heaped up in regards to You.

How could Christ have broken them down on the cross, if—as I believed about him then—he had been a phantom on it? As false as his death seemed to me then, so true was the death of my soul. And as true as the death of his flesh is, so false was the life of my soul that was not believing in it. My fever was rising, now I was on my way to death. But where would I have gone, if I had departed from here back then, except into the fire and into torments fitting for my deeds in the truth of Your order? (*Conf.* V, 16)

Reflecting in the *Confessions* how and why he went to Rome, Augustine observes that at that time he would have given a perfectly rational account for leaving Carthage. In the African capital, long-established custom permitted students to run wild, to the great detriment of whatever order the teachers labored to establish in their classrooms. No such license was granted young scholars in Rome: They were not allowed to barge into classes where they were unenrolled. Thus Augustine's move to the great city on the

Italian peninsula—now no longer the capital of the Empire—appeared to be motivated by these secular ambitions for a more pleasant work environment. Yet when he looks back upon this move, he confesses that it was God working by means of various stimuli—a carrot and stick approach—to get him to Rome "for the salvation of my soul." God's will was an undertow, working below all the secondary factors that he would then have claimed were the reasons for the move. Human beings, people in love with this mortal life, were the immediate promoters of his decision. The boisterous students at Carthage who had driven him from there were "blinded by their foul frenzy" and totally unconcerned for the spiritual state of their harried instructor. Those promising a better situation for Augustine at Rome also had their minds fixed on things of the earth. Yet these exciting causes brought him closer to the spiritual homeland as he left his native country. This is the way of divine Providence, which works where people are in order to get them where they need to be.

Augustine's time in Rome was marked by his almost fatal sickness and his recovery to the remnants of his old life. Even at death's door, Augustine confesses that he had no desire for Catholic baptism. Although lodged in the house of a generous Manichean host, his heart was not there, for he had already lost all hope of finding Truth—God—from that source. Yet he had not resolved the questions that originally led him to favor the Manichean way. The Manichees had the wisdom to reject any notion that God was in human form like the gods of Greek and Roman mythology—and Augustine always agreed. He had also liked their approach to the question of the origin of human sin. The Manichees, like many gnostic groups, found fault not in the individual's will, but in an extrinsic factor: matter, and the body itself drawing us willy-nilly into sin.

For it still seemed to me that it was not we who sinned but some other nature in us—I know not what—that sinned. It pleased my pride to be beyond blame, and not to confess myself to have done it when I had done something morally wrong. Had I confessed it, You would have cured my soul, since it was a sinning against You. But I loved to excuse myself and to accuse something else—I don't know what—that was present with me, yet was not what I was. In truth, however, I was my whole self; and it was my impiety that divided me against myself. But it was a deeply uncured sin by which I judged myself not to be a sinner. It was a cursed iniquity, O omnipotent God, to prefer You to be overcome in me for the sake of my ruination than for me to be overcome by You for the sake of my salvation. But You had not yet set a guard on my mouth and a gate of self-control around my lips, so that my heart would

> not incline toward wicked speech aimed at making
> excuses for sins done in the company of people who
> were workers of iniquity. So I was still keeping com-
> pany with their Elect, although I had now given up
> hope of my making progress in this false teaching. I
> had decided that if I found nothing better, I would
> be content with these teachings, although I now held
> on to them in a rather careless and slack manner.
> (*Conf.* V, 18)

Another factor kept Augustine from thinking that the
church could offer truth. Although he still thought of God
as some kind of physical reality, Augustine did not imagine
God to be bound to the form of a human body. It was
preferable to conceive the divine nature as an infinite mass
of a shining and glorious substance, limited only by
another such cosmic substance—but an evil one. This
opposing entity he likewise pictured as an infinite substance, "having its own mass, either foul, misshapen, and
dense (which the Manichees called earth), or rarefied and
subtle like the body proper to air, which they imagine to be
an evil mind creeping throughout the earth." Augustine
felt it impious to attribute the existence of such an ugly and
evil substance to God, so he embraced the Manichean
explanation that both these masses—of Good and of Evil—
originally existed independent of each other. Thus they had
gotten mingled only after they fell into combat. Equating
evil with matter led him to reject the notion that Christ
could have been born of the Virgin Mary. For if Christ
were incorporated in the flesh, how could he not have been
contaminated by it? Neither Augustine nor his fellow
Manichees would accept this, because for them Christ was
the Savior come down from the world of light to free us
from the bondage of the powers of darkness and the prison
of the body.

Augustine's growing detachment from the Manichees was accompanied by an attraction to a school of philosophy he knew from Cicero. These philosophers were called Academics because they were Platonists who maintained that they were the true successors of Plato's Academy in Athens. The Academics claimed that the true philosophy must hold to Socrates' way of philosophizing. This famous philosopher, who had died for his beliefs, was a relentless skeptic and questioner. Socrates was more inclined to show the problems in other peoples' theories than to construct systems of his own. Because the Academics emulated the Socratic suspension of belief, Augustine preferred them to the other schools of philosophy or religious thinking that confidently asserted their own way was truth. He found a salutary modesty in the Academic adoption of the principle, "that one ought to exercise doubt in all things and that nothing true can be definitively grasped by human beings." The mistake of Mani, after all, had been his rash assurance in teaching as certain a variety of doctrines, some of which were contradicted by known science. Others were of a purely mythical nature and thus not in any way self-evidently true.

Approving this doctrine of universal skepticism, Augustine also began to feel that the Catholic teachings were not quite so ill-defended against Manichean criticism as he had earlier supposed. In Carthage he had heard a Catholic spokesman, Elpidius, dispute publicly with Manichees. Privately, they had assured Augustine the problem lay in the "fact" that the Catholic New Testament (which the Manichees also reckoned to be of some authority) had been corrupted by some people "who wanted to graft the Jewish law onto the Christian faith." Yet when challenged by Elpidius, the Manichees were unable to produce any uncorrupted copies, so their attempt to respond fell short. But what really began to push Augustine in the direction

of the Catholic fold was his move to Milan. Despite his hopes for better working conditions in Rome, the students there had their own bag of tricks. Not as blatantly devilish as the Overturners at Carthage, they were disturbing in their own way. Private teachers, such as Augustine was at Rome, were paid by the pupils at the end of each term; this arrangement provided the students with the opportunity to hear Augustine's lectures and then bail out at the end of the semester without paying him! Small wonder that when an official, salaried appointment as professor of rhetoric in the imperial capital of Milan was offered to him, Augustine jumped at the chance. Ironically, Augustine was recommended to the prefect of Rome for this position by his Manichean friends, his disillusionment with the sect notwithstanding. The prefect of Rome was a wealthy and learned orator named Symmachus, who was an enthusiast for the traditional Roman religion. Scholars have speculated that it may have amused Symmachus to send to Milan, home of the famous bishop Ambrose, a Manichee professor of rhetoric—a heretical Christian.

Heretic or not, Augustine was welcomed in Milan by the bishop, Ambrose, who had a great reputation as an orator. It was a providential meeting of minds, for although they never became intimate, Ambrose demonstrated to Augustine that the church could interpret Scripture with intellectual integrity. Employing an allegorical method of interpretation, Ambrose showed that the stories of the Old Testament patriarchs had a deeper spiritual meaning beneath the surface of the historical narratives in which they appeared as rather compromised saints. This manner of reading religious texts had been developed in the centuries before Christ by Stoic philosophers troubled by the way Homer had depicted the Greek gods acting in immoral ways. These moralizing educators sought to make these poems, which were the basis of Greek education, suitable reading for impressionable young minds. It's ironic that a method of reading developed by pagan thinkers for their own religious concerns should prove to

be the key that opened Augustine's vision to the insight that the highest spiritual truths could be found in the full canon of Christian Scripture.

Although unaware of it, I was led to Ambrose by You, in order that I might be led through him to You. That man of God received me in a fatherly manner and demonstrated the kind of loving concern, appropriate to a bishop, for my travels. I began to love him, at first not indeed as a teacher of the truth—since in fact I was still unable to have any hope in Your church—but as a person who was kind to me. I eagerly went to hear him hold forth publicly, not with the purpose which I ought to have had, but just to check out his ability, to see whether it matched his renown and whether he spoke with more or less fluidity than had been claimed of him. I hung rapt upon his words, but I remained disdainful and uninterested in what he was talking about. . . . Although I did not bother to learn about what he was saying, but came only to hear how he was saying it (this empty interest remained to me, even though I still had no hope that a way to You might be open to human beings), along with the speaking that I loved there also came into my mind the subject matter that I was ignoring—for I was unable to separate them. And as I opened my heart to absorb how learnedly he was speaking, there entered equally the sense of how truly he spoke, though indeed this was a gradual thing. For it began to seem to me for the first time that these things could be defended. I started to think that the Catholic faith, in defense of which I had maintained nothing could be said in opposition to Manichee attacks, could be asserted without embarrassment. This happened most of all when one and another of the puzzles from the Old Testament rather frequently came to be solved. These passages were places which, when I accepted them literally, killed me. Consequently, when many passages from these books had been interpreted spiritually, I started to criticize my lack of hope, by which up to this point I believed the law and the prophets could in no way be upheld in the face of those people who despised and mocked them. (*Conf.* V, 23–24)

Ambrose's preaching removed for Augustine the obstacles that stood in the way of his accepting the faith. He no longer considered it vanquished by Manichean arguments, but was yet to regard it the victor. Adopting the stance of the Academic philosophers with their canny refusal to grant assent to what was uncertain, Augustine refrained from signing up fully with any philosophers who "were without the saving name of Christ." What then did he do? Strangely for one whose religious doubts had by no means been put to rest, Augustine resolved to take up where he had left off as a boy: "so I decided to be a catechumen in the Catholic church which had been commended to me by my parents until something certain should cast light upon where I should direct my course."

CHAPTER SIX

Treading Water: Worldly Goals of a Suffering Soul

My hope from my youth, where were You for me? Where had You gone? Isn't it true that You made me, and that You distinguished me from the four-footed beasts and from those that fly the sky? And didn't You make me wiser than them? But I was walking through shadows and a slippery place, seeking You outside of myself—and I was not finding the God of my heart. And I came onto the depths of the sea, despairing and losing hope about finding truth. My mother, strong in her piety, had now come to

me, following me over land and sea, in all perils
secure about You. Even over the watery reaches she
was consoling the sailors themselves, by whom inex-
perienced sea-travelers are accustomed to be con-
soled when they get upset. She promised them a safe
arrival, since You had promised her this in a vision.
Me she found imperiled, quite gravely, indeed, from
my loss of hope about discovering truth. Still, when
I had indicated to her that I was in fact no longer a
Manichee (though not a Catholic Christian), she did
not hear it as something expected. She didn't leap
for joy either, since she had already become secure so
far as my unhappiness was concerned. . . . Her heart
did not pound with turbulent exultation, despite
having heard that the thing had happened, the thing
she wept over daily to You that it might be accomplished. I had not yet arrived at the truth, but I had
been pulled away from falsehood. More still, since
she was certain that You who had promised the
whole thing were going to deliver it, she responded
to me in the calmest fashion, her heart full of faithfulness, how she believed in Christ that before she
departed from this life, she would see me a faithful
Catholic. (*Conf.* VI, 1)

In the face of such a mother's calm assurance, how could
Augustine ever have disappointed her? She had laid a heavy
trip on him—no exaggeration. But we must beware of mis-
conceiving Augustine's theological conversion as a purely
psychological drama where his feelings of guilt and obligation toward his mother play the main role. Without deny-
ing that these factors were operative, we must match the
pace of our understanding to the story the *Confessions*
unwinds. At this point Augustine still has a long way to go,
all his mother's divine assurance notwithstanding. The why
and the how of his conversion are the subject matter of

books VI through VIII. Speaking of Augustine's "conversion," we must keep in mind that we are referring to something he depicts as a long process, not a single event. A series of turnings has now brought his life back into the Catholic church, if only in a provisional manner. Ambrose's allegorical readings of the Old Testament removed a number of difficulties, but did not bring to Augustine a clear conception of God as an immaterial spirit. Thus he began the process of entering the church without fully understanding God's nature. His decision to renew his status as a catechumen in the Catholic church signaled that he suspected truth was more likely to be found there than anywhere else.

Book VI of the *Confessions* is devoted largely to the people in his life in Milan: his mother; Ambrose; and two friends from Africa, Alypius and Nebridius. Alypius, a former student of Augustine's, was also from Thagaste and was the son of a wealthy man. Nebridius too came from a well-to-do family, from around Carthage. Alypius had been in Rome, and he had followed Augustine to Milan. Nebridius joined them there so they could live a philosophical life together. When we think of Augustine's life in Milan, we have to imagine him as the central figure in a group of fellow Africans including his two good friends, his wife-of-sorts, his son, his mother, and sometimes other relatives. Augustine was quite busy teaching rhetoric, along with the occasional demand to deliver a speech for state celebrations. Contrary to this picture of a settled life, the real topic of this book is the clear onset of change. Augustine recounts a number of transitions undergone by his mother and his friends. He himself appears on the brink of a transition. The old life and the old hopes for worldly success are still very much with him in the person of his mother, busy in the social circles of Milan arranging a society marriage for him. Being on an upwardly mobile track, thanks to his education and talents in rhetoric, Augustine could anticipate marrying into a higher class and a monied family. Once that was obtained, he could head for the next rung: an appointment to an imperial office in some distant province. Such an appointment would elevate him to a higher social class, probably to the lowest rung of the senatorial order. This traditionally hereditary order had recently developed a number of levels to accommodate people promoted to that class by virtue of official position or imperial favor. But however firm this trajectory may have been in his and his mother's minds, it was not where God was leading Augustine.

Monica, for her part, had to undergo some adjustments. Augustine records his amazement at her willingness to drop her old religious practices after learning they were not allowed in Milan. She had been accustomed to bringing food-offerings to the martyrs' memorial shrines. But when she brought her gifts of porridge, bread, and wine to the cathedral, the doorkeeper blocked her entry, because Ambrose had forbidden this way of honoring the martyrs. The practice of bringing food and drink to the shrines was dicey on two counts. Those who came to celebrate at the martyrs' graves were known to indulge too heavily in the wine they brought to toast the faith's departed heroes. Augustine also notes that this feasting at their graves resembled a little too closely the traditional pagan practices of "feeding" the dead. His chief point in telling the story, however, is to show how love for another person can bring a change in one's own life. Although Monica had never taken more than a sip in celebration of the martyrs, she readily embraced Ambrose's orders in this matter. For the sake of Ambrose, and for what he was to her son, Monica quietly adopted the customs of the new church, which

entailed merely a celebration of prayer in place of the customary offerings.

> But, O Lord my God, it nonetheless seems to me . . .
> that my mother would perhaps not have easily given
> way in this custom she had to abandon if she had
> been prohibited by a different person, one she did
> not love as much as Ambrose. She loved him so much
> for the sake of my salvation. And he indeed loved her
> for her extremely religious manner of life, which set
> her spirit so on fire that she often went to the church
> and did good deeds. Thus when Ambrose saw me, he
> would very often break out in praise of her, congrat-
> ulating me on having such a mother. He was unaware
> what sort of son she had, one who was in doubt
> about all these issues and who maintained that the
> right way of life was probably not discoverable.
> (*Conf.* VI, 2)

The extent of Augustine's spiritual problems remained unknown to Ambrose. Augustine and his friends used to try to get a good sit-down with the bishop to talk about their spiritual questions. But when they arrived at his office, they saw how the bishop used his free time for reading, and so hesitated to interrupt him. They knew what a busy man he was and how precious that time of study was to him. Ambrose's influence was exerted less through personal contact and more through preaching, which presented Augustine with a method for reading troublesome parts of the Bible. Allegorical interpretation was applied to the Scriptures by many Christians under the explicit recommendation of the apostle Paul. Augustine was delighted to hear Ambrose constantly preaching Paul's words to the people: "for the letter killeth, but the spirit giveth life" (II Cor. 3:6; KJV). The removal of Augustine's difficulties with the Old Testament, however, did not resolve all his questions, because many of them were of a philosophical nature and demanded a high level of discussion. Influenced by philosophy and its standards of proof, "I wanted to be as certain of things I did not see as I was of the fact that seven and three are ten." This left him miserably stranded, all the while becoming more and more conscious of his misery.

> I was gasping after honors, riches, and marriage—
> and You were mocking me. In pursuit of these
> desires I was suffering the bitterest difficulties. The
> more well-disposed You were, the less You permitted
> me to enjoy any sweetness that was not You. . . .
> How unhappy I was, and how You dealt with me so
> I would feel my own unhappiness on that day when
> I was preparing to deliver a speech in praise of the
> emperor! Amidst those praises I would lie a great
> deal; and approval would be bestowed upon me as I

lied by those who were cognizant of the fact. My heart was wheezing with these cares and burning with the fever of my languishing thoughts. Passing by on one of the streets of Milan I noticed a homeless beggar, drunk already—I believe—joking and happy. I groaned and talked to the friends with me about the many sorrows of our mad pursuits, since in all our attempts we wanted nothing else than to reach a sure happiness. The beggar had already reached that place, but we were perhaps never going to get there. For he had obtained his goal with just a few begged coins; and toward this same end, the joy of an obviously temporal happiness, I was pounding the pavements of my miserable rounds. Not that he had true joy, but that I was seeking joy much more falsely by those ambitions. Yet he was enjoying himself; I was full of anxiety. He had a sense of security; I was fearful. (*Conf.* VI, 9)

Even when he was pursuing his career and marriage, Augustine knew that no true happiness could come from wealth and position. Couldn't he have both worldly success and a Christian life? Here we have to stretch our theological and historical imaginations to understand why Augustine felt it was such an "either/or" situation. Part of the answer lies in the fact that he understood the Christian calling as a call to a "philosophical" life. This meant a life designed to be as simple as possible, and free from external demands. Only this would permit Augustine and his friends to devote themselves fully to the pursuit of wisdom, because they were not from wealthy enough backgrounds to avoid careers and their cares. The pursuit of worldly success, however, required a diversion of his time and attention to a multiplicity of demands—and this did not permit the singlemindedness demanded by the search for wisdom, as he then conceived it. This conflict between spiritual goals and the necessities of life comes poignantly to expression in a long passage where

Augustine takes stock of himself and his failure to follow through on the insights he had gained from his "first" conversion, the conversion to philosophy. That book of Cicero's had set him on fire with a zeal for wisdom and had kindled in him a desire to cast away all worldly cares.

> As I attended to my memories, I was most of all amazed about how long a time it had been since I was nineteen and had begun to burn with a passion for wisdom. Once that was discovered, I would abandon all empty hopes for futile desires. Now look: carrying on at thirty and stuck in the same mud, owing to my eagerness to enjoy the fleeting things of the present which were scattering me all over! All the while I was saying, tomorrow I will make a discovery. See, the truth will appear clearly and I will lay hold of it. See, Faustus will come and explain everything. The Academics were great men! Nothing certain can be grasped about how life ought to be lived. No, let us search more diligently and not give up hope. See, the things in the church's books that seemed absurd no longer seem absurd; they have a different and acceptable way of understanding them. I'll put my feet on the path where as boy I was set by my parents until some evident truth be found. But where does one search for it? And when? Ambrose has no leisure, nor is there leisure for reading. . . . Students take up our mornings—what shall we do with the remaining hours of the day? Why don't we get on with it? But when will we make social calls on our influential friends, whose recommendations we need? When are we to prepare what our pupils are paying for? When are we to refresh ourselves by giving the mind a break from its focus on tasks?
>
> Let all these concerns perish, let's drop all these meaningless and empty pursuits, let's devote ourselves only to the search for truth. Life is unhappiness, death

can come at any time and take one suddenly from behind. What will be the manner of our departure from here, and where will we learn the things that we have neglected here? And isn't it likely there will be damages to be paid for this negligence? What if death itself cuts off awareness and puts an end to all our worrying? So this too must be an object of inquiry. No, far be it that this should be the case. Life is not meaningless, it's not in vain, since so great and high an authority accrues to the Christian faith spread throughout the whole world. So many such things wouldn't be divinely done on our behalf, if the life of the soul too would come to an end with the death of the body. So why do we hesitate to devote ourselves totally to seeking God and the happy life, once all hope in the world has been abandoned? But wait—things here are pleasant and have no small sweetness of their own. . . . An abundance of powerful friends are available; we should press forcefully with no other aim than to obtain a governorship of a province. I ought to marry a woman with some money, so that the necessities of life would not weigh too heavily on us. That will be also be a way to maintain our lustful desires. There are many great men, most worthy of imitation, who have given themselves to the pursuit of wisdom in a married state. (*Conf.* VI, 18)

Augustine was suffering from cognitive dissonance. He knew a better way but refused to reach for it, for he had not yet given up on his old hopes. This inner conflict was one thing that made him different from the beggar. The beggar's happiness—not a true happiness—was unmarred by any such conflict regarding a higher goal of happiness. Not so with Augustine, who was at a loss as to how he might bring his life into accord with his own best knowledge, with his own higher self. This is the tension that proceeds the transformation that will take place only after he comes to a feverish pitch of despair about all his good, but impotent, resolutions. His experience of entrapment, which he often likens to being stuck in mud, glue, or some sort of snare, led Augustine to meditate deeply upon the way we can have selves—or aspects of our self—in conflict. But before he lets his readers into the secret of how he was released, Augustine prepares us with a story of his friend Alypius and the transformation he underwent under the guidance of the secret Providence of God.

Alypius had studied with Augustine in Carthage. He had always appeared to Augustine to be a virtuous young man (indifferent to the pleasures of sex), but this student had nonetheless become much addicted to the races. At the time, Augustine was not in a position to correct his errant ways, which seemed to pose a threat to his making progress in his studies for a career at law. There had been a falling out between Augustine and Alypius's father, who had forbidden his son to study rhetoric with the Manichee professor. But as time went by, Augustine realized that Alypius did not share his father's opinion of him. Alypius began to frequent his lectures again. During one of these lectures, Augustine was explaining a passage in some text and reached, as teachers often do, for a contemporary illustration. Without a thought for Alypius's situation, Augustine used as an example the circus-games (chariot races, not gladiatorial combat), and with biting mockery spoke of the madness that captures those who frequent the race-courses. Although he hadn't the slightest intention of addressing Alypius's situation, Alypius took it to heart, "believing that I had said this only on his account." A person of lesser integrity, Augustine thinks, would have been enraged at him; but Alypius was enraged at himself and his habit, and loved Augustine all the more for what seemed to be a concern for his welfare. Augustine found the incident a superb illustration of a saying from the book of Proverbs: "rebuke a wise man and he will love thee" (Prov. 9:8; KJV).

But the story doesn't end there. If it did, we would be left with the impression that people retain the ability to correct themselves with a little external prodding. To prevent such an impression, Augustine relates what happened to Alypius when he got to Rome and trusted too much in his own strength and good intentions.

> There Alypius was unbelievably seized with an unbelievable gaping after gladiatorial shows. For although he opposed and despised such things, certain of his friends and fellow-students, whom he met by chance as they were returning from dinner, led him by

friendly violence to the stadium during the days of the cruel and sinister games. He protested forcefully and resisted, saying, "if you drag my body to that place and set it down there, you don't really think you can bend my mind and my eyes to those shows, do you? I'll pay no attention, and thus I will overcome both them and you." Having heard this, they led him off with them all the same, perhaps wanting to find out whether he could hold to it. When they arrived and had been seated, the whole place was frothing with brutal pleasures. Shutting the gates of his eyes, Alypius laid his mind under the injunction not to attend to such things. If only he had also closed his ears! At a knock-down in one fight, when a giant roar of the whole crowd struck him hard, he was overcome by curiosity. Thinking himself prepared to despise and overcome it even while viewing it, whatever it was, he opened his eyes. He too was struck, but with a wound in the soul, graver than what the fighter had received in the body, the wound he'd craved seeing. Alypius had fallen more miserably than that man whose falling had raised the roar. It had entered through his ears and unbarred the way to the lights of his soul. There he was struck and thrown down, his mind more daring than it was strong. He was weakened to the extent that he had presumed to go it alone, when he ought to have depended on You. For when he saw the bloodied fighter, he drank in brutality at that moment; he did not turn himself away but gave it his attention. He imbibed madness and was unaware of it. He was delighted by the accursed combat and became intoxicated with the gory pleasure. He was no longer the same person who had come there, but was one of the mob to which he had come, truly a comrade of those by whom he had been led off. How much more! He looked on, he shouted, he became embroiled, he carried off insanity with him from there. It motivated him to return, not only with those by whom he had been taken, but he went beyond them in dragging others there too. Nonetheless, You rescued him from that place by a far stronger and most merciful hand, and You taught him to have confidence not in himself but in You—but that came long afterward. (*Conf.* VI, 13)

Important to Augustine's point is the fact that Alypius was not a vice-ridden youth but actually a young man of great promise and virtue, as a further story makes clear. During his early career in the law at Rome, Alypius held a position that afforded him a certain amount of power in some important matters. One case in particular opened him to corruption and thus gave him the opportunity to live out the kind of virtue he aspired to. A powerful and wealthy senator offered him a bribe for a favorable outcome in a legal case. The presiding judge was willing to look in the other direction and let the great man have his way; not so Alypius. His refusal of a bribe elicited threats, which also made no impression upon his virtuous character. Augustine pointedly relates another incident in which Alypius refused to take advantage of his government position and have books copied, for his private use, at a much reduced rate. This temptation, especially for a book-lover, must have been considerable, yet Alypius turned it down for the sake of justice.

Augustine includes these stories about Alypius because of their theological content. Too often, good and decent Christians have a superficial view of sin and think that a wayward life and an addiction to sinful practices are the prerogative of persons who are outwardly and evidently depraved. The challenge is to understand how sin can be a controlling power even in the lives of those who are not clearly unregenerate—and this is precisely what Augustine wants his readers to know.

Augustine's passion, unlike Alypius's, was not something that had overcome him all of a sudden, and it was not to watch gladiators or chariot races. Augustine seems to have felt about sex in the way many people feel about addictions. His sexual habit, however, was an addiction—perhaps like all addictions—that he was not ready to give up. He clearly loved and appreciated the sexual relationship he had with his long-time partner. If he thought of trading that in for legitimate marriage, Alypius raised the objection that matrimony would be an impediment to their leading the philosophic (meaning, Christian philosophic) life. Citing examples of great married philosophers, Augustine countered that Alypius failed to appreciate the difference between his limited, furtive, and all-but-forgotten sexual experience and the "regular enjoyment of my habit." Add to that enjoyable habit the honorable names of matrimony, and pursue wisdom at the same time—not an option to be lightly rejected! Augustine must have been quite convincing on the topic of the compatibility of marriage and philosophy (a traditional philosophical conundrum), because Alypius himself became interested in marriage. "He was overcome," Augustine wryly observes, "not by the desire for such a pleasure but by curiosity about it." Alypius claimed to be merely eager to know just what that thing was, without which, Augustine said, "my life did not seem like a life to me but a punishment."

For a variety of reasons, then, Augustine was headed for marriage. Both he and his mother had put quite a bit of effort, and much hope, into it. Monica connected his marriage with his getting baptized shortly thereafter, as he appeared to be moving progressively in that direction. She was so concerned about the whole thing that she daily prayed for God to give her a vision about the marriage—and God did not oblige. Finally the arrangements were made, and the engagement was on, but it would be a long one. The girl was quite literally a girl: she was two years away from the legal age (which was eleven or twelve in Rome—something that shocked Greeks, who felt that a girl should reach puberty prior to marriage), so Augustine would have to wait. But he had to get rid of the woman he been living with in order to become engaged, and that devastated him. Now true misery was upon him, and this came as no surprise. He had previously taken stock, maintaining "that I would be unhappy beyond measure were I to be deprived of the embraces of a woman." Two years of such deprivation until his fiancée came of age was too much for Augustine to bear, so he went out and found himself an interim girlfriend.

In the meantime my sins were multiplying. The woman with whom I was accustomed to sleep was torn from my side as an impediment to the marriage. My heart, clinging to her, was struck hard and wounded within, and it left a trail of blood. She returned to Africa, vowing to You never to know another man. Left behind with me was the son born from her of my flesh and blood. But I was unhappy and not an imitator of the woman: impatient with the delay (as I was to take the girl whose hand I had sought only after two years), I got another woman. I did this because I was not a lover of marriage but a slave of lust. By no means did I take her as a wife, only as a means to maintain the disease of my soul and prolong it intact, or livelier, in submission to a hardened habit till it reach the estate of matrimony. That wound of mine which had been inflicted by the slicing away of the previous woman was not healing; rather, after the initial boiling over of pain it was getting more deeply infected. Frozen over in a way but more despairingly, it continued to give me pain. (*Conf.* VI, 25)

Anyone who has ever broken up with someone under the weight of necessity can probably relate to Augustine's feelings. But set in the context of his life, there is not merely the pain of a break-up to deal with but also a painful irony of his spiritual malaise. Just when Augustine appears on the verge of getting what he wants—a wife with money—he is tipped into a more intense state of despair by an unavoidable loss, into a depth of pain he had not reckoned with. He and his friends were still searching for wisdom, although without any conclusive result. Their plans to pool their money, live communally, and take turns attending to worldly matters to free the rest for spiritual pursuit all came to nothing. The plan ran aground on the fact that their wives would not tolerate such an arrangement. Augustine himself struggled with the idea that perhaps the ancient philosophers who dedicated their lives to enjoying themselves (the Epicureans) were in fact the wisest. Only his inclination to believe in the immortality of the soul prevented him from signing up with their doctrine. For if there is something more to life than the pleasures of the present, a full and lasting happiness must obviously take account of something higher.

CHAPTER SEVEN

Light Upon Light: Encounter with the Books of the Platonists

The rejection of error does not entail a grasp on the truth. Book VII of the *Confessions* picks up with Augustine still unsure about the nature of God, but having decided on the Catholic church as the most likely home of truth. Because he knew that God was an incorruptible substance and therefore clearly to be preferred to anything corruptible, the error of Manichean theology appeared more glaring. Augustine is now convinced by an old argument of Nebridius (from their Carthage days) against the Manichean creation story. If God is inviolable—a belief they take all pious people to hold—why did God have to defend against the attack of the world of Darkness and sacrifice a part of the divine to be swallowed up by those forces? If God cannot suffer harm, this self-sacrifice was surely unnecessary. The Manichees, Augustine thought, could not evade this dilemma. If they held God to be violable, "the falsity is obvious and to be rejected at a first hearing."

Augustine was revising his opinions in other areas as well. His attachment to astrology was also fading. So far, it had withstood the attack of the wise old doctor Vindicianus as well as the repeated, if less assured, assaults of Nebridius. Nebridius had always argued that chance guaranteed a certain percentage of the astrologers' forecasts would be true, yet Augustine had never been fully swayed. An incident involving a friend who wanted Augustine to draw up his horoscope tipped the balance. Firminus was a well-born and well-educated man who was zealous for astrology, although without Augustine's practically expert knowledge. He consulted Augustine about the variety of readings astrologers had offered him on questions pertaining to his worldly fortunes and ambitions. Augustine confessed that such things now appeared to him "absurd and meaningless"—and this provoked a story from Firminus that was to drive the final wedge between Augustine and astrology.

Firminus's father was an enthusiast for this occult art, along with a good friend and neighbor. Both men avidly observed all the births on their lands: those of their family, slaves, and animals. At the time of Firminus's mother's pregnancy with him, a slave belonging to the neighbor was also pregnant. Both seemed equally far along. The two men arranged to monitor the exact time of birth and notify each other. At approximately the same time, the two women went into labor. When the babies were born, each man dispatched a messenger to inform the other—and the messengers met at the exact midpoint between their estates! The stars, of course, were in identical positions for the births of both children. Yet each was destined to grow up to a completely different fate, one to be a slave and the other a master. This story convinced Augustine that the position of the heavenly bodies can neither predict nor determine events. He found this point confirmed in the biblical story of the twins Jacob and Esau. Augustine then abandoned astrology, and he was one step further from error and closer to the truth.

Augustine needed enlightenment on two key points: the nature of God and the source of evil. The question concerning the origin of evil brought yet another issue to the fore: What is the relation of the human will to evil? Is evil inflicted on the will, something outside itself that forces the best part of us to submit? As a Manichee, Augustine had believed that a part of the divine was imprisoned within us and subjected to the evil matter from the world of Darkness. Having rejected the Manichean picture of the world with its two eternal and opposing forces, Augustine was left disturbed, having no clear answer on the subject. Ambrose may have sketched the Catholic position, but apparently he did not demonstrate the matter to Augustine's satisfaction. But he could not fully accept the faith until his mind felt settled about the nature of God and the origin of evil.

> I bent my mind to comprehend what I was hearing: that the free choice of the will was the cause of our doing evil, and that it was Your just judgment that we suffer. But I wasn't up to seeing the point clearly. Although I tried to bring my mind's discerning power up out of the depth, I sunk down again. Often I tried, and again and again I sunk down. For I was working to lift myself up into Your light, because I knew I had a will just as well as I knew that I was

alive. Since I was extremely certain that it was none other than I who willed or did not will when I either willed or did not will something, I now looked there for the origin of my sin. Now, what I did unwillingly I saw myself to suffer rather than to do; and I came to the conclusion that this was not itself a fault, and I confessed it rather to be a punishment by which I was not unjustly beaten, knowing immediately that You were just. But I started saying again, "Who made me? Wasn't it my God, who is not only good but Goodness Itself? Where then does my willing evil and non-willing of the good come from? So that there would be a reason for me to justly suffer punishments? Who put this in me, who sowed this plant of bitterness, if I have been altogether made by my God, the most sweet? If the devil is the author of it, where did the devil himself come from? Because if it was on account of his twisted will that the devil himself was made out of a good angel, from where did the evil will in him,

by which he became the devil, come from when it was
as a totally good angel that he had been made by the
best creator?" By this line of thinking I was brought
down and suffocated, although I was not led down to
that hellish depth of error where no-one confesses to
You, preferring to maintain that You suffer evil rather
than that human beings commit it. (*Conf.* VII, 5)

Many people find the question concerning the relation
of God to evil a difficult and thorny thicket. Christianity
traditionally affirms the omnipotence of God, human free
will, and the reality of evil. What you think about one issue
frames the manner in which you conceive the others.
Augustine never seriously considered the possibility that
God could do evil, because this conflicted with his rock-
bottom intuition about the nature of God. This intuition
was something pagans could agree with. Plato himself had
stated this conclusion in *The Republic*: God does no evil
(379b). But a simple affirmation of this statement does not
clear up the issue, at least not for those given to wanting
logical explanations. To say that God does no evil just
affirms that God is good, or is Goodness Itself (as Augustine and others influenced by Platonism would say); but
one has not yet said exactly what the nature of God is. Is it
enough merely to say what God is not? If whatever is must
be some kind of substance, then what kind of body is God,
given that God would have to be a different kind of body
than we see in the bodies of created things?

I was raising the question of where evil came from,
but I was seeking evilly and didn't see any evil in my
questioning. I would set up in my spiritual vision the
entire creation and whatever one can picture in it—
land, sea, the air, the stars, trees, and mortal beings—
and also what we cannot see in creation—the

firmament of the heavens, all the angels, and all other spiritual creations in it. Also those things that are physical my imagination ordered in appropriate places. I mentally set up, as Your creation, one immense mass, distinguished within by the kinds of beings, whether real physical ones or those I had imagined in lieu of spiritual realities. I made it immense, not of a specific size but immense beyond compare, although finite on all sides. You, O God, ran through it and penetrated it in every way, You being absolutely infinite. It was as if the sea were everywhere, pure infinite sea in all directions through magnitudes of space, and the sea contained within itself a sponge as large as possible but still finite. That sponge would surely be full in every part with the enormous sea. This was how I was thinking of Your creation: finite, and filled with You who are infinite. I was saying, "Look—this is God! Look—God's creations! God is good, far and away more excellent than they; but being good, God has created good things. And look—how God runs through them and fills them! So where is room for evil? And why has it crept in here? What is its root and what is its seed? Or is it altogether non-existent? Then why do we fear it, and why are we on guard against what does not exist?" (*Conf.* VII, 7)

For all his restless and inquiring spirit, Augustine was not seeking God in the right way. He was looking for God in the wrong place and looking at wrong models of existence. He looked toward created forms as a model for the being of God. The corporeal images that filled his mind obscured his vision. Not only external factors hindered his sight. His pride also got in the way. Augustine's sense of himself as an expert in the forms of outward things (his first book was entitled *On the Fitting and the Beautiful*) prevented him from looking within, the road that finally, but not yet, would lead him to an understanding of spiritual reality.

For I was superior to these corporeal things but inferior to You. You are my true joy, when I am subject to You; and You had subjected to me the things You created that were beneath me. Now this was the right balance and the middle region of my salvation: that I would remain in Your image and be master of my body while serving You. But when I proudly rose up against You, and ran up against the Lord with the thick neck of my shield [see Job 15:26], even those things that had been made lower than me came to oppress me, and there was never any rest or breathing space. These things were coming at me from all

sides, piled up and clumped together in my attempts to discern them. These images of bodies fell upon me as I turned back, as if someone were saying to me, "where are you going, unworthy and dirty creature?" All this had grown out of my wound, because You bring low one who is proud but wounded. And I was separated from You by my swelling; my swollen face itself was closing over my eyes. (*Conf.* VII, 11)

Yet God had mercy upon Augustine, "earth and ash" as he confesses himself to be. God, he writes, "reformed his deformities" and goaded him to further inquiries until the divine nature was a reality he could be certain about. He found his "swelling" subsiding under the influence of God's hidden hand that served the right medicine at the right time. His mind was being "healed from day to day by the salve of health-bringing woes." The "healing" refers largely to his intellectual problems, the main one being his inability to conceive the reality of God except along the lines of material things. The healing of his sexual addiction would come later. His intellectual infirmity was healed through the reading of some books of philosophy that fell into his hands at the right moment. Because Christianity is a religion of the book, it is no surprise that his conversion came about through reading. But what he read was not the Bible, nor even a Christian book. His misunderstanding about the nature of God was removed and replaced with a better understanding thanks to what he read in pagan philosophical writings.

Not that every Christian of Augustine's world would easily accept the notion that these books could contain knowledge of God. Sensitive to this perspective, Augustine presents the fruits of his reading of these philosophical books alongside a careful comparison with Scripture. He explicitly notes where the agreement with the pagan philosophy begins and ends. He introduces, moreover, his reading of these books with a delicious irony in which the humble way of Christ is compared to the lofty pretensions of pagan philosophy: "Wanting to show me how You 'oppose[s] the proud, but give[s] grace to the humble' (1 Pet. 5:5), . . . through a certain man who was swollen stiff with monstrous pride You procured for me certain books of the Platonists translated from the Greek language into Latin."

We know from another work of Augustine's composed at the time that these books included a few short writings of a philosopher named Plotinus. Plotinus was a native of Alexandria, Egypt, who had lived and taught in Rome in the middle of the third century. Modern historians of philosophy regard him as the first Neoplatonist. By this term scholars mean that Plotinus's Platonism had been deeply influenced by other schools of philosophy (by Aristotle and by the Stoics) and presented an original synthesis. One of the most important features of this synthesis was a certain mystical strain. By "mystical," I mean that Plotinus was not content just to analyze reality conceptually. Rather, he sought to experience ultimate reality in a way that went beyond what is generally called "thinking." Plotinus held a deep conviction that the soul was a mobile thing, capable of sinking to the lower levels of life as well as ascending to the highest, to God. This ascent of the soul to God, as practiced by Plotinus, involved the mind going beyond itself. The mind has to go beyond its normal mode of knowing, where the knower is separate from what is known. Ideas of "mystical union" with God are not foreign to Christianity, but the way Plotinus conceived the goal of philosophy is different from how any Christian would ever phrase it. "Our pursuit," wrote Plotinus, "is not just to exist without sin, but to be God" (*Enneads* I, 2, 6). This went too far for Augustine, who maintained the Bible's clear line of distinction between God the Creator and all creatures. However much Augustine may have learned from Plotinus, he was also concerned about marking off what was pagan in spirit from what was compatible with Christian truth.

> Having been advised by those books to return to myself, I entered into my deepest parts with You as my guide. I was able to do this, because You are my helper. I entered, and with whatever sort of eye my soul possessed, I saw the unchanging light which was above that same eye of my soul, above my mind. It wasn't normal light, the kind visible to all flesh, nor was it something grander of the same sort—as if such

a light would shine brighter and brighter and take up the whole sky in size. This light was not that kind but something different, very different from all the lights of that sort. And it wasn't above my mind the way oil floats on water or the sky is above the earth. Rather was that light superior to my mind because it made my mind. I was inferior to it because I was made by it. Those who know the truth know that light, and those who know that light know eternity. Love knows the light. O eternal truth, O true love, O beloved eternity—You are my God! I sigh for You day and night! When I first came to know You, You took me up to see that the BEING I saw was real, and that I who saw was not that BEING. And You smacked down the weakness of my gaze, blasting me heavily with light. I trembled with love and awe, and I found myself in a land of unlikeness. It was as if I were hearing Your voice from on high: "I am the food of grown-ups: grow and you will feed on Me. And you

> will not change Me into you, like fleshly food, but
> you will be changed into Me." . . . I said to myself, it
> couldn't be the truth is a nothing just because it is
> not diffused through either finite or infinite space.
> And You called out from afar, "rather is it truly I Who
> Am the One Who Is." I heard it as one hears some-
> one in the heart, and there was no further recourse
> for doubt—I would more easily doubt that I lived
> than that truth existed, the truth that is "made visible
> and understood through the things that have been
> made" [Rom. 1:20]. (*Conf.* VII, 16)

Augustine had seen the light and heard the word of
God. This was a true breakthrough. He had experienced
God as real in a far more concrete way than ever before.
What he saw seemed compatible with what he knew from
the Bible. Hadn't God told Moses the Divine name,
declaring "I AM WHO I AM" (Exod. 3:14)? Didn't the
opening of John's Gospel state that "in the beginning was
the Word, and the Word was with God, and the Word was
God," and that all things were made through the Word?
The precise language of the Gospel is not exactly dupli-
cated by Plotinus, but Augustine saw the same thought
present. Yet there were things from Scripture that he knew
were not in the philosophical books, chief among them
being the fact of the incarnation: that the Word became
flesh and dwelt among us. From these books, Augustine
got something that didn't require any revising in light of
Scripture: a vision of a reality that was not physical in any
way, not just matter in a rarefied or concentrated form.
God was not a being like other beings, only greater; God
was BEING, and differed as much from other beings as
that invisible light I saw differed from all creaturely light.
(The use of capitals symbolizes God's BEING as unlike
that of every other being, whose defining characteristics

constitute limitation—for example, I am a human being, not an angel or an aardvark; American, not Canadian; male, not female; and so on.) That BEING which is God is the source of whatever other limited existences there may be; and that light from BEING is the source of the knowledge which all those creatures created with understanding possess. Once Augustine understood that BEING of God—that God is the very power of being—he also grasped the relation the creatures bore to the One who had created them good. And that solved his problem with the question of evil, at least on the theoretical level.

> It became clear to me that everything which is corrupted is good. For they wouldn't be able to be corrupted if they were not good, or if they were the

highest good. If they were the highest goods, they would be incorruptible; and if they weren't at all good, they wouldn't contain anything which could be corrupted. For corruption causes harm; and unless it threatens to damage some good, there would be no harm done. So either corruption harms nothing (which can't be the case), or—what is most obvious— all things that are corrupted are deprived of a good. Now, if they were deprived of every good, they will in no way exist at all. . . . Therefore, whatsoever things exist are goods; and that evil whose origin and being I was seeking was not a substance. . . . In regards to You I saw that no evil exists at all; and that is the case not only for You but for the whole of Your creation, since outside of it there is nothing that could break in and corrupt the order which You have laid upon it. Now, in parts of it there are certain things reckoned as evil because they are not fit for certain other things. Yet these very same things fit other things and are good for them and for themselves. (*Conf.* VII, 18–19)

This is Augustine's famous solution to the problem of evil in the universe. Once you establish that existence in itself is a good, even though a particular existence may be a miserable sort (say, on death row, or in the throes of a painful and incurable disease), then you can't conceive evil as some force independent of existing things. It is only because God creates that evil is at all possible; for without any creation, where could evil be? Evil does not exist as such. It arises on the level of creatures, something for which God cannot be blamed. Once God is established as a spiritual substance of unchanging existence and goodness, Who nonetheless creates beings capable of change (which is what it means to be part of creation, because what is created comes about in the first place by a change from non-existence), then there is no need for the Manichean view of

an evil substance responsible for the evil in creation. This means that evil must be chalked up to the will of humans and other spiritual creatures. Thus Augustine's solution also provides a justification of the ways of God.

> On the basis of what I had learned, I realized it is no wonder that the bread that is sweet to a healthy person is torturous for the taste-buds of the sick, and that light is odious to sick eyes while it is beloved to healthy loves. Even so does Your justice displease the wicked, just as do poisonous snakes and grubs . . . I

129

also searched to see what wickedness was, and I did not find a substance but the twisted turnings of a will that has been torn off from the highest substance—You, O God—and sent to the depths, hurling forth its inner parts and swelling outwardly. I marveled that I was now loving You, not a phantom in Your stead, and I did not hesitate to enjoy my God. Rather, I was grasped to You on account of Your beauty but was soon grabbed away from You by my weight, rushing into you-know-what and groaning all the while. This weight was my fleshly habit. But the memory of You stayed with me, nor was I in any way doubtful about that BEING to whom I would stick. The problem was that I was not yet such as could stick, because "the body which is corrupted weighs down the soul, and the earthly dwelling oppresses the mind as it thinks many things" [Wisdom of Solomon 9:15]. (*Conf.* VII, 22)

It is one thing to know the truth about evil abstractly and quite another to be cured of the evils caused by one's corrupting turns of the will. Unlike Plotinus, Augustine's ascent of the mind to God ended with the revelation that he was not such as could perceive that BEING, because he was himself in a sorry state, "a land of unlikeness." At least this is how he describes the culmination of that vision in the *Confessions*, written over a decade after the event. Although the books of the Platonists had granted him sufficient vision of truth to be sure that God existed and was infinite, he confesses he was turned back at the height of the vision. Still, the vision allowed him to sense "what I was not permitted to behold on account of the dark areas of my soul." So it was a mixed experience, yet at the time it gave rise to a great feeling of pride in himself, which he does not fail to mention and condemn.

I babbled on and on as if I were an expert. Yet if I were seeking Your path in any way but in Christ our Savior, I would be no expert but about to expire. For I had begun to want to appear the wise man, though full of my punishment which I was not bewailing. Besides that, I was getting puffed up with knowledge. Where was that love which builds up from the foundation of lowliness which is Jesus Christ? When had those books taught me that? I believe this was the reason why You wanted me to run into those books before I took consideration of Your Scriptures: so that it would be impressed upon my memory how I was affected by these books and—after I was tamed by Your books and my wounds had been touched by Your healing fingers—so that I might discern and distinguish what was the difference between presumption and confession, between seeing where one must go, though not seeing the way, and seeing the way

131

that leads to the happy homeland which is not only to
be observed but dwelt in. (*Conf.* VII, 26)

Augustine even thinks that if he had first grown familiar
with Scripture and then read the philosophical books, they
might have "torn him away from the solid ground of piety"
or, at least, led him into the delusion that a healthy state of
being could be obtained through them alone. It's clear that
Augustine was very impressed by the vision of reality in
them. But the pagan philosophers counted among the
forces of resistance to Christianity, both before and after the
conversion of the emperor Constantine. Some of the Neo-
platonists (for example, Plotinus's greatest pupil Porphyry)
attacked Christianity in writing but found an honorary place
for Christ in their pantheon of gods, heroes, and deified
human beings. At the time Augustine was reading those
Platonist books, his view of Christ was remarkably similar to
that of these pagan philosophers. He believed that Christ
was a human being whose wisdom was greater than that
offered by all others. He interpreted the virgin birth as a
means God employed to teach us to despise all temporal
things for the sake of gaining immortality; it was God's way
of vesting authority in Christ's teaching. Augustine confesses he did not grasp the mystery of the Word made flesh.
His friend Alypius, who did believe that in Christ God had
put on flesh, later learned that his understanding of the
incarnation (he maintained that with the flesh, God did not
also take on a human soul or mind) was heretical. Augustine discovered this later through the teaching he received
in the church while preparing for baptism. After the
encounter with the books of the Platonists, Augustine
turned again to the Scriptures. The apostle Paul taught him
that the damage wrought by sin remains with us even when
the saving faith of Christ has been grasped.

Thus I greedily grabbed the venerable composition of Your spirit, primarily the apostle Paul. All those problems vanished, passages where his writings had formerly seemed to me both to be in self-contradiction, and not to agree with the witness of the law and the prophets. The face of chaste eloquence appeared to me, and I learned to rejoice with trembling awe. (*Conf.* VII, 27)

CHAPTER EIGHT

Converting Conversions

Book VIII of the *Confessions* describes the decisive moment of Augustine's conversion. It came in a garden under a fig tree, where the strength of his feelings had sent him away from all human company to be alone with God. We do not know exactly what transpired in those moments, but it was surely something that would now be called "a decision for Christ." But the problem with labeling his experience in this fashion is that we may end up obscuring its specific character. It is clear that Augustine intended to depict the events as a moment of illumination, bringing him the resolve he had always found lacking in himself. This moment, however, involved both a break and a continuity, paradoxical though that may sound. This is consistent with the general picture he gives us. Augustine presents his life as a process, a series of turns, for good and for ill, all of which have so far been incomplete. A notable transformation in his relation to the church had already occurred prior to the decisive moment. He had accepted the universal church as the bearer of truth, and he had begun to make forays into Scripture. Even before the decisive event, Augustine was "converting" toward the official form of Christianity, although he wasn't yet freed from the burden of his sin. He'd taken steps in the right direction, but had further to go.

To tell his own story, Augustine must relate the stories of other people that moved him along the way. Learning about other people's conversions was essential to his own conversion, which in reality was a series of events leading up to what one could call the big event. But this long process, which we can as a whole entitle "conversion," did not stop with the last of the events recorded in the *Confessions*. The Augustine who wrote this book was not the same Augustine he was writing about. In the meantime, he had gone through much, read and thought much. The moment of transformation under the fig tree—some scholars have with good evidence argued—has been heavily colored by his deepening reflections in the interim between the event and the writing about it. Careful studies have shown how his views on grace evolved during this period, particularly regarding the role of the human will in salvation. His notion of grace at the actual time of conversion included a cooperative effort on the part of the human person. After more intensive study of the Bible and particularly Paul's letter to the Romans, Augustine arrived at a more profound view of grace in which the human will, cooperative though it may appear in the struggle for salvation, actually contains a deep well of resistance to God. This "bondage of the will" (a phrase Luther used to describe the same phenomenon) is a way of talking about what the apostle Paul meant in Romans by the phrase "a law of sin in my members." Around the time of his conversion, Augustine thought this phrase referred to human beings as they are "under the law" (that is, prior to the faith of Christ). But after his deeper meditations upon Scripture, he came to understand that the "law of sin"

remains present even after the reception of grace. This will be a point that he illustrates in book IX, when he discusses how erotic dreams still disturb his soul after that moment of conversion.

> O my God, in giving thanks to You let me recall and confess Your mercies upon me. Let my bones pour forth with Your love and let them say, "Lord, who is like You?" [Ps. 35:10] You have broken my bonds, I will offer a sacrifice of prayer to You. I will relate how You broke them; and let everyone who worships You say when they hear this, "blessed be the Lord in heaven and on earth: great and marvelous is God's name!" Your words had stuck in the folds of my heart and from every side I was hedged around by You. I was certain about Your eternal life, although I had but seen it "in a riddle," "through a mirror" [1 Cor. 13:12], as it were. But all my doubts about an incorruptible substance—that from it all other substance would come—were removed. It wasn't that I wanted to be more certain of You but rather to be more stable in You. Now, in regards to my temporal life everything was wavering, and my heart needed to be purified from the old leaven. The path—the Savior himself—was pleasing, but going through his narrow way felt laborious. You put it into my mind, and it seemed good in my sight, to go see Simplician, who looked like a good servant of Yours to me, someone in whom Your grace was shining. (*Conf.* VIII,1)

Unlike Ambrose, Simplician was a man to whom Augustine could unburden himself and relate "the circuitous routes of my error." Hearing that Augustine had just read the books of Neoplatonist philosophers, Simplician commended him, because "God and his Word were shot through and through in them." Other philosophical books might have led Augustine down another erring path, but these contained sound truth, despite the actual religious allegiance of their pagan authors. These books had been translated from Greek into Latin by Marius Victorinus, a learned and famous teacher of rhetoric who had late in life converted to Christianity. (This had happened to the great chagrin and surprise of the pagan aristocracy, which had just awarded him the rank of senator and erected a statue in his honor at Rome.) Like Augustine, Victorinus was from Africa; and the road to Rome was for him a road of professional success and social betterment. But unlike Augustine, he was at the end of his career when he became a Christian, around the year 355, about the time of Augustine's birth. Augustine had in fact heard of him and—significantly—knew that he had died a Christian. Besides their professions, the two men shared an avid interest in philosophy and an approach to religion that saw it closely linked to philosophical questions about the good life and the nature of reality. Augustine notes that Simplician told him the story of Victorinus, "in order to exhort me to the lowliness of Christ which is hidden from the wise and revealed to little ones." The story moved him at the time, and later it provided material for his own meditations on the mystery of God's grace in converting even enemies of the faith. For up until his conversion, Victorinus had been "a worshiper of idols and a participant in sacrilegious solemnities." Augustine, of course, had never been a pagan, but he too had to undergo a great deal of searching and personal transformation before he could bring himself to enter the church.

> O Lord, Lord . . . what were the ways in which You wound Yourself into that heart? Victorinus was reading—as Simplician said—the Holy Scripture and all

Christian writings, analyzing them closely. He was saying to Simplician, not openly but in a private and intimate manner, "you may know that I am now a Christian." And he responded, "I won't believe it, nor will I consider you among Christians unless I see you in the church of Christ." But he laughed it off, saying "so—it's the walls that make Christians?" He used to say this often, that he was now a Christian; and Simplician often gave him that response; and often the joke about the walls was repeated by him. For he was afraid to offend his friends, proud demon worshipers . . . and he was thinking that their hostility would rush upon him heavily. But afterward, by reading and breathing it in, he drank down resoluteness. He came to fear being denied by Christ before the holy angels, if he appeared ashamed about the sacraments of the lowliness of Your word, and not ashamed about the sacred sacrileges belonging to proud demons which he had accepted as a proud imitator of them. He lost his shame in regards to the empty thing and became ashamed in the face of truth. Suddenly, and in an unexpected manner, he said to Simplician (as he himself told it), "Let's go to church: I want to become a Christian." And Simplician, losing hold of himself for joy, went with him. There he was endowed with the first sacraments of instruction, and not much after he submitted his name to be reborn through baptism. While Rome was struck with wonder, the church rejoiced. The proud looked on and got angry, grinding their teeth they faded away. But the Lord God was the hope of Your servant, and he took no regard for their empty nothings and crazy lies. (*Conf.* VIII, 4)

Simplician's story of Victorinus's conversion set Augustine on fire to imitate him. Yet he held back, torn between competing desires, unable to make a decision for a new way of life. Augustine thought the old professor fortunate in the way an external occasion had propelled him to give up his chair of rhetoric for the sake of his faith. For in the year 361, Julian the Apostate (the only pagan emperor after Constantine) attempted to turn the Roman Empire back to paganism. Toward this end, Julian issued a law that only adherents to the traditional religion of the empire could occupy the state-supported professorial positions. Faced with this ultimatum, the newly baptized Victorinus did not hesitate to abandon his means of livelihood and public position. No such external stimulus presented itself to Augustine. What held him back from a conversion were his worldly habits, which could be maintained only if he continued in his professional career. He was experiencing in his own life what he had been reading about in Paul's letter to the Galatians: "the flesh lusteth against the Spirit, and the Spirit against the flesh" (Gal. 5:17 KJV). Augustine felt two wills within him: a new one, recently inspired to abandon the world and give himself to God and the pursuit of wisdom; and his old one, a will that would not give up on the worldly desires that had been motivating his whole adult life.

Anyone who has ever experienced deep inner conflict can relate to Augustine's experience of having a divided will. The experience is not uncommon, whether it be an addiction one would like to kick, or an unhappy sort of love one cannot bring oneself to abandon even when a better life beckons on the other side of what would nonetheless be a painful loss. The mind's inability to command its own will deeply puzzled Augustine. If our conscious self makes a decision, why can't we follow through on it? Augustine answered this question with a couple of considerations. On the one hand, there is the force of habit. He began to see our difficulty in breaking long-accustomed ways of being as a fitting penalty for the sins so long tarried in. On the other hand, he also realized that due to our creatureliness and the presence of sin, our selves are not whole. We are all fragmented in one way or another. Augustine provides us with numerous experiences from everyday life to confirm this picture, even humorously trivial ones.

> Thus was I sweetly oppressed by the burden of the world, like someone sleeping. The thoughts I was thinking about You were like the efforts of those who seek to wake themselves from sleep but sink back

again, overcome by the depth of their sleep. Although no-one wants to sleep all the time, and all sound judgment prefers to be awake, people often delay shaking off sleep, especially when there is a heavy slug over the whole body. Even though the time to get up has come, sleep plucks one off, protesting, though readily giving in. The case was thus: I was certain it were better to give myself to You than to give way to my lust; the first way pleased me and was winning out, but the latter pleasured me and entwined me around. (*Conf.* VIII, 12)

But why did his "decision" to give himself to God mean giving up the planned marriage? We moderns, more than his original audience, have a hard time relating to Augustine's asceticism, his philosophy and practice of self-control. But the connection between Christianity and a preference for the virginal or celibate life was not something he or his generation manufactured. Christian asceticism traces its origins to the practices of Jesus and Paul, who were themselves both celibates. By Augustine's time, this strain of religiosity was in full bloom. Italy began to imitate the developments in the deserts of Egypt and Syria with the establishment of ascetic communities. Augustine and his friends, unaware of the fact that there was a monastery in nearby Milan, had been contemplating individual or small group ascetic practice. Despite the tradition of philosophers pursuing wisdom in the married state, Augustine does not seem to have regarded this as an option.

> I saw that the church was full: some lived one way and some another. But my problem was that I was carrying on with life in the world. Bearing up with so burdensome a job was a heavy load, since there were

no longer those former burning desires of hopes for honor and money. No longer did these things delight me beyond Your sweetness and the beauty of Your house, which I loved. The problem was that I was still tightly linked to a woman. It wasn't that the apostle had prohibited marriage, although he did exhort us to something better, most of all wanting all people to live the way he did [see 1 Cor. 7]. But I was the weaker and chose a more comfortable place. It was on account of this one thing that I went round and round, lazy in some matters and wasting away with professional obligations. Along with other things I did not want to suffer, I had to put up with these in order to fit the bill of married life. Having surrendered myself to it, I was bound by it. I had heard from the mouth of truth that there were those who had made themselves eunuchs for the sake of the kingdom of heaven—but it said "let those accept this who can" [Matt. 19:12]. (*Conf.* VIII, 2)

Augustine also recounts here the conversion story told him by a fellow African, a man named Ponticianus. He was a Christian, albeit employed as a special agent at the imperial palace in Milan. Dropping by to visit Augustine and his friends, Ponticianus was surprised and delighted to find a book of Paul's letters lying open on a gaming-table. He then proceeded to unwind the story of St. Antony's conversion. It was so well-known among Christians that Ponticianus couldn't believe Augustine and friends hadn't heard it.

The temptations of St. Antony are perhaps the most famous part of the hermit's life, because many know him only through the numerous paintings of his temptations. The story of his conversion is tied to the beginnings of Christian monasticism; communities of ascetics grew up in the wake of his decades of solitary or anchoretic practice. Antony, the son of an Egyptian farmer, walked into church one day and heard the Gospel being read: "go, sell your possessions, and give the money to the poor, and you will have treasure in heaven; then come, follow me" (Matt. 19:21). And he did just that, putting aside enough to support his sister. At first Antony followed the practice of an old hermit from his town, living in a little shed on the outskirts. Soon he began withdrawing deeper and deeper into the desert, where he finally took up residence in a deserted fort and locked himself in. The ancient *Life of St. Antony* tells of all the demons that attacked him with many temptations and in various guises. But Antony clung to God in prayer and defeated them all. After twenty years of solitude, many people had been drawn to his isolated hermitage from a desire to see the celebrity; unable to contain themselves any longer, they broke down the door. When Antony emerged, the crowd was amazed to see him in perfect health, his body neither emaciated nor flabby but with the perfect appearance of Adam before the fall. Hearing the call of duty, Antony left his beloved solitary life and rejoined the civilized world to do healings, route devils, and debate heretics before withdrawing again. Antony and the monastic movement set out an ideal of Christian commitment: a willingness to follow Jesus as his first followers did, leaving their families, possessions, and jobs. This definition of the Christian ideal was a large part of the reason why Augustine and others like Ponticianus felt it impossible to both maintain a career and commit themselves to God. It seemed like serving two masters.

Ponticianus then went on to relate his own story. He and three other officers in the imperial service were with the emperor in Trier (now in Germany). The emperor was completely caught up in the chariot racing, which gave

Ponticianus and his friends the opportunity to take a walk in the woods. Off they went, walking and talking in pairs. Two of the men happened upon a dwelling of monks. There they found a little book describing the life of Antony. As they read it, they became incensed at themselves and their professional aspirations.

> Tell me now, where are we trying to get to with all these labors of ours? What are we looking for? Why are we in the military? Do we have any greater hope at court than that of being "Friends of the Emperor"? Is there any place there that is not provisional and full of danger? And through how many dangers will we have passed to get to this greater danger? And when will this be? But to become a friend of God—look, I can do that now if I want! (*Conf.* VIII, 15)

Casting his eyes back on the book, the man read on, and as he did he was changed within, where God alone sees. Inwardly resolved, he declared his intention to his comrade,

who also decided from that very moment to drop his worldly career in dedication to the service of God. When Ponticianus and the fourth friend rejoined the new converts, they wept with joy at their friends' decision but in sorrow at the fact that they could not follow, but would return to their careers and families.

> This was the story Ponticianus told. But amidst his words, O Lord, You threw me back to look at myself, taking me from behind my back where I had put myself when I didn't want to look at myself. You set me before my face so that I would see how unfit, how contorted and filthy I was, how blemished and covered with sores. I took a look and was horrified, and there was nowhere to flee from myself. But if I tried to turn my mind away from how I seemed to myself, there was Ponticianus telling that story. And You kept putting me in my face, forcing my eyes to see myself, so that I would discover my evil and come to hate it. I had acknowledged it, but was keeping up a pretense, repressing it and forgetting it. (*Conf.* VIII, 16)

The more Augustine listened and admired the two men whose conversions Ponticianus told, the more he came to hate himself as he was. After a dozen years of deferring his decision to pursue wisdom and throw off the world, he was just as unhappy as at the beginning of his resolve when he had prayed, "give me chastity and self-control, but not now." He had long justified putting off his decision on the grounds that he hadn't found certainty yet. But this excuse was now gone, so his conscience snarled at him. Hadn't he discovered something certain? So why was the earthly load still oppressing him? Others had cast off the yoke—why not he? Ponticianus's story caused Augustine to be "horribly ashamed" of his lack of progress toward his own ideals.

When the man departed, he lashed out at himself. Alypius stared in wonder at the outward manifestations of the great inner struggle.

At that moment amidst the great strife of my inner house, which I had aroused against my own soul in the inner chamber of my heart, my face was as distraught as my mind. I burst out at Alypius shouting, "What are we putting up with? What is this? What did you just hear? Uneducated people are rising up and taking hold of heaven, while we with our bloodless learning, look, we're tumbling around in flesh and blood! Or is it so shameful they got there first that it is not shameful not to follow at all?" I said some such things; and my heated temper tore me away from him, while he kept silent and stared at me in astonishment. For I did not even sound like myself. My forehead, my cheeks, my eyes, my complexion, and the tenor of my voice expressed my mind more than

the words that I brought forth. There was a certain garden that belonged to our lodgings. . . . The tumult in my heart brought me there, where no one could get in the way of the burning struggle I had embarked upon with myself until there should be an outcome. How it would come out—You knew, O Lord, but I did not. All I knew was that I was sanely raving and dying full of life, knowing what my evil was but unknowing what was soon to be my good. So I retired into the garden, and Alypius followed in my footsteps. . . . How was he going to abandon me in such a state? We sat as far away as we could from the building. I was raging in my spirit, indignant with an extremely perturbed indignation, because I would not enter into an agreement and a compact with You, my God, into which all my bones were crying out for me to go and lifting up their voices of praise to heaven. And one did not get there by ship, carriage, or feet: it was not even as far as I had gone from the house to that place where we were sitting. For not only to set out, but also to get there took nothing other than willing to go. But it required willing forcefully and fully, not with a half-sick will, now hesitating, now bounding forward, one part rising to struggle while another part falls. (*Conf.* VIII, 19)

In looking back at his struggle in the garden, Augustine reaches an understanding of his problem and why he was unable back then to resolve it. At the time, he tore out his hair and gripped at his knees, doing all the things people do when in deep inner conflict. What a strange thing that the mind can command the body and receive almost instant obedience but cannot do the same with itself! This was a phenomenon that the Manichees had explained with their hypothesis of two minds, two wills, or two opposing substances within human beings. But now Augustine had discovered a better explanation. The will itself is divided, and one is literally at conflict with oneself. There only seem to be two wills, "because one of them is not complete, and what is present to one is absent from the other." In this case, what was absent from his good will was the power to bring his intentions to actuality. One foot went forward and the other went back. He was "hesitating to die to death and to live to life," and yet that was what his better side wanted.

His old habits were not totally out of commission, however. They plucked at his flesh and whispered to him: "Are you really going to get rid of us? From this moment on are we going to be apart from you forever? From this moment on will you never be permitted to do this or that again?" Augustine was ashamed by the mention of the "this or that," which his old desires tried to pull him back with, but the strength of their objections was not what it used to be. Though not totally deprived of voice, they could merely murmur at him in a lukewarm manner. Christians of both sexes appeared so much stronger than he was in that moment. Shame rose up again in his heart.

When my deep self-examination drew forth and gathered together from its hidden bottom my whole unhappiness in the sight of my heart, a huge tempest broke out, bringing with it a huge shower of tears. In order to let them flow along with their cries, I rose up from Alypius's side; solitude seemed more appropriate to me for the business of weeping. I withdrew further, so that even his presence might not be burdensome to me. This was my state of mind then, and he sensed it. Something I had said before, I don't know what, had made it apparent that my voice was heavy with weeping, and so I arose. He, therefore, remained where we were sitting and was quite dumbfounded. I cast myself under some fig-tree (I don't know how) and let go the reins on my tears. Rivers burst forth from my eyes, a sacrifice acceptable to You. Not, indeed, in these words but with this thought I said many things to You, "Lord, up until what point, up until what point will You maintain Your anger till the end? Do not remember our ancient evil-doings." For I felt that I was held fast in them. I threw unhappy cries about: "how long, how long will it be tomorrow, tomorrow? Why not now? Why not let this hour be the end of my vile behavior?" (*Conf.* VIII, 28)

Augustine's struggle was almost over. What precipitated the decisive change is something that scholars still debate, for Augustine's account suggests a mysterious intervention.

Lo and behold, I hear a voice from a neighboring house. A song is being recited and repeated, like the voice of a boy or girl, I don't know which: "Take up and read, take up and read." My mood immediately changed, and I began to contemplate very intensely whether or not children were accustomed to chanting

any such thing in some kind of game. I couldn't at all remember having heard it, and I got up, the impact of my tears having been checked. I took the meaning to be none other than that I had been divinely commanded to open the book and to read the first verse I found. For I had heard about Antony that he had been summoned by a reading from the Gospel that he had by chance come upon. What was being read seemed to be spoken to him: "Go, sell all you have, give it to the poor and you will have treasure in heaven, and come follow me" [Matt. 19:21]. By such an oracle, I had heard, he converted to You without delay. Greatly aroused I returned to the place where Alypius was sitting, for I had set the book of the apostle down when I had gotten up from there. I grabbed it, opened it and silently read the verse which my eyes first hit upon: "Not in revelry and drunkenness, not

> in chambering and shamelessness, not in strife and
> envying, but put on the Lord Jesus Christ and make
> no provision for the flesh" [Rom. 13:13-14]. I nei-
> ther wanted nor needed to read further. Immediately
> with the end of that sentence, a light, as it were, of
> certainty poured in my heart and put all my shadowy
> doubts to flight. (*Conf.* VIII, 29)

What decided his will at that moment, what rendered his
divided self whole? Certainly his will was suddenly enabled,
where previously it had been disabled. But whether Augustine enabled his own will, say, by a resolute choice, is
entirely another question. The fact that he attained this resoluteness in a sudden encounter with a scriptural verse relevant to his difficulty suggests God's gracious power.
Augustine implies this with the phrase "a light, as it were,
of certainty poured into my heart." This light of certainty
eliminated all the shadows, all the unknowns that had been
between him and a new life. It would have been obvious to
his audience that God was the mover of these events, especially with the mysterious children's song leading to the
discovery. Augustine also depicts his encounter with a
"chance" verse as a well-trod road to conversion, hence his
mentioning that the story of St. Antony was in his mind.
This is how people are converted: by hearing the word of
God, the way God speaks.

Alypius, too, heard God speak through that encounter.
When Augustine showed him the verse in chapter 13 of
Romans, he read the next line and applied it to himself:
"Receive someone who is weak in faith." He resolved to
follow Augustine's example forthwith, seemingly without
struggle. Augustine thought his was because Alypius's
nature had always been more inclined to the good. So in
Alypius's case the conversion seems more like an act of will;

but the question still remains: why then? Everything that led up to it was a series of events in which Augustine and his friends were searching and not finding. Now, when Augustine was struck out of the blue, Alypius was drawn in as well, drawn in by the divine web that was out there in so many ways they were unaware of. It was not a matter of their suddenly facing a pure up or down decision, a yea or nay—for they were precisely nay and yea. Rather they were brought to a point where there was no going or looking back. It happened, the shadows were banished, and it was time to get on with a new life.

CHAPTER NINE

Deaths and a New Life

The final portion of the *Confessions* that can properly be called autobiographical is book IX. It ties up the story by telling the aftermath of the conversion, both the events leading up to Augustine's baptism and those afterward culminating with the death and burial of his mother. Augustine informs us about his state of mind after the garden revelation, how he was angry with the Manichees, and how at the reading of the Psalms he wept with profound love of and gratitude toward God. But the center of book IX is Monica. This is partly because she died just as they were about to sail back to Africa, but there are other reasons as well. In this book, Augustine tells us that by divine grace, he and his mother were granted a vision of God. He also relates several incidents in Monica's life, all of which depict the grace of God working in, by, and with the sins of human beings. God's grace, of course, is the central thread that runs through the *Confessions*.

> "O Lord, I am Your servant, I am Your servant and the son of Your handmaid. You have broken my bonds, I will sacrifice to You an offering of praise" [Ps. 116:16-17]. Let my heart and my tongue praise You, and let all my bones say, "O Lord, who is like You?" Let them speak, answer me, Lord, and say to my soul, "I am your salvation." Who am I, and what sort of person? Is there any part of me not involved with evil? My deeds? No. The things I've said? No. My will? No. Yet You, O Lord are good and merciful: Your right hand had regard for the depth of my death and drained the abyss of corruption at the bottom of my heart. The whole thing is this: not to want what I was wanting, but to want what You were wanting. But where was my free choice for so long a stretch of years? From what deep well, from what hidden depth was it called forth in a moment, so I might submit my neck to Your light yoke and my shoulders to Your light burden, O Christ Jesus, my helper and my redeemer? (*Conf.* IX, 1)

The first issue Augustine faced after his decisive conversion was how to resign his professorship. He felt like dropping it immediately, but feared that doing so would seem like ostentation, "as if I had wanted to look like a great man." So he decided to keep the matter of his change of mind private, to share with his friends and family, and to resign from his professorship only at the end of the term. He could put up with the twenty days left until the fall break, knowing that his time of teaching from the "seat of lies" was almost at its end. Because he had been having some lung trouble, and his voice was strained, he could offer that as a plausible reason for his resignation. He would displease the parents of his students, but they would accept it. Augustine's desire to keep his departure from the world low-key may strike us as an excess of modesty, but it is explicable for religious reasons. Augustine knew that there were Christians around who would have applauded an immediate and uncompromising break with the world. Although he agreed with them in principle that it was a sin to tarry in this regard, he seemed to fear more making his conversion into a public and political show. Perhaps he was influenced by Jesus' sayings in the gospel that we should pray in private and not make a public spectacle of our relationship with God.

In the fall and winter of the year 386, Augustine, his friends, and his family stayed at a friend's country estate near Milan. Verecundus, a Christian who deeply regretted being unable to take up a celibate way of life (as Augustine and Alypius had done), was happy to make his country home in the village of Cassiciacum available to them. The timing was fortunate, for Verecundus's generosity provided a quiet place of withdrawal for his friends as they prepared for their baptism that coming Easter. Augustine wrote a series of dialogues to record the kinds of conversations he was having with his friends there. These writings (*On the Happy Life, Against the Academics, On Order, Soliloquies*) show that Augustine was working out some of the solutions to his theological problems. Because these works were written at the time of the conversion, scholars have eagerly compared them with his later writings that date from the time of the *Confessions*. This has led to some controversy concerning when and how Augustine made a full conversion. None of these dialogues relate the story of the garden and that earth-shaking passage of Scripture, so some have suggested that Augustine really converted to Neoplatonism with only a slight tincture of Christianity. But there are a number of problems with this thesis and some evidence to the contrary. Most significant is Augustine's self-depiction in the book *Soliloquies*. The opening of this little work contains a prayer that breathes much of the same spirit as the *Confessions*. Augustine presents himself as a sinner who would be unable to progress at all without the help of God—and much of it is couched in the language of the Pauline epistles.

From his account in the *Confessions*, we also get a sense of his Scripture readings in preparation for baptism. Ambrose had advised him to read the book of the prophet Isaiah, perhaps because the Gospel is most nearly foreshadowed in that book. Augustine, however (and this may be a comfort to those of us who find parts of the Bible to be difficult going), found the opening impenetrable and did not feel confident about continuing to read when he hadn't understood the beginning. So he put it away, assuming that the time would come when it would be accessible to him. At that time he did study the Psalms, that great source for Christian spirituality of all times. Perhaps the psalmist's deeply personal language of love and longing, the cries of humble spirits aware of their sin, spoke to his heart.

> How I cried out to You in the reading of the Psalms! How I was set on fire for You by them and how inflamed I was to recite them, if I could, to the whole world against the pride of the human race! And yet they are sung through the whole world, and none can hide themselves from Your heat. How angry with heavy and bitter sorrow I was at the Manichees; and on the other hand how I pitied them, since they were

ignorant of the medicinal sacraments and were madly
raving against the antidote by which they could have
been cured! I wished that they were somewhere
nearby then and—without my knowing that they
were there—that they could have looked upon my
face and have heard my cries when I read the fourth
psalm in that time of my leisure. (*Conf.* IX, 8)

It is a tribute to his humanity that Augustine would still
think about those comrades in his path of error, that he
would wish that they could see and understand him now.
Many of his writings in the coming decades would aim at
the refutation and correction of their false views. However
much Augustine saw them as snared in error, he knew from
personal experience that in their own minds they were
seeking truth. Their mistake was not reckoning that God
had provided the church as the historical vehicle both for

the transmission of the truth and for healing in this life and the next.

Little surprise that Augustine's son, Adeodatus, joined his father and Alypius in baptism. Adeodatus's mother, who had been sent away, may very well have been a Catholic Christian (not a Manichee). Augustine had educated his son (as one might expect from a professor) and probably also involved him in his quest for truth. That the boy was frighteningly smart we may surmise from his father's loving description of his gifts. Adeodatus's sudden

death shortly after their return to Africa must have been a tremendous sorrow for Augustine, although the *Confessions* conceals that grief.

> When the time came for me to hand in my name for baptism, we left the country and returned to Milan. It seemed good to Alypius to be reborn to You with me in baptism, already clad in a lowliness appropriate to Your sacraments. He had become a most impressive tamer of his body, to the point where he went barefoot in the Italian winter, something not done. We also took Adeodatus along with us, who was begotten in a fleshly way by me and from my sin. You made him well. He was almost fifteen years old, and in intelligence he surpassed many seriously learned men. I am confessing Your gifts to You, O Lord my God, creator of all things, power to transform our deformities—for in that boy I had no part beyond my transgression. No one but You inspired us to let him be nourished by us in Your teaching. I am confessing Your gifts to You. There is a book I wrote which is entitled *On the Teacher*. Adeodatus himself converses with me in it. It is his thoughts when he was sixteen—You know—that are put in there in the person of my interlocutor. I experienced many more incredible things on other occasions: that intelligence of his seemed awesome to me. Who besides You can work such marvelous things? You took away his life quickly from the earth, and I call him to mind now with a greater degree of security, having no fear for him about anything occurring during his teen-age years or early adulthood. We took him with us as a peer in Your grace to be brought up in Your teaching. We were baptized, and all our concern about our previous lives fled from us. (*Conf.* IX, 14)

At this time Augustine's other great friend, Nebridius, was still in the process of making a transition from Manicheism to the Catholic faith. Augustine and Alypius had great hopes for his eventually following them, and in this they were not to be disappointed.

> Nebridius was rejoicing along with us. Not yet a Christian, he too had fallen into that pit of pernicious error, such that he believed that the flesh of Your true son was a phantom. At length emerging from that, he was in a state where he had not yet been dipped with any of Your church's sacraments, and yet he was a most ardent seeker of truth. Not long after our conversion and rebirth through Your baptism he also became a faithful Catholic, serving You in Africa with complete celibacy and self-control among his own people, since his whole family had been made Christ-

ian through him. Then was he released from the flesh, and now he lives in the "bosom of Abraham" [Luke 16:23]. Whatever that may be which is signified by "bosom," there my Nebridius lives, my sweet friend but Your son, Lord, adopted into freedom: there he lives. What other place would befit such a soul? There he lives on, in the very place that he so often questioned me about, me, an inexpert little man. No longer does he put his ear to my mouth, rather he puts his spiritual mouth to Your fountain and in his eagerness drinks as much wisdom as possible, his happiness knowing no end. I don't think he would get so intoxicated from it as to forget me—since You, O Lord, whom he is drinking, are mindful of us. (*Conf.* IX, 6)

Augustine's loving testimony to Nebridius witnesses to his assurance about eternal life with God. First, there is his faith that Nebridius is indeed with God (in "the bosom of Abraham," as Luke's gospel puts it in the parable of Lazarus and the rich man). There is also here a conviction that what one enjoys in that life is none other than God. This sense of assurance about those who have gone before was important to Augustine, especially because he experienced the loss of so many loved ones: first Monica, then his son, then Nebridius. He suffered these deaths differently than the much earlier death of his boyhood friend. Now he is a Christian, so his faith in the resurrection affects the way he experiences death. Christian thinking regards the death of the faithful as tragic, humanly speaking, but not final. This does not mean that Christians do not grieve—something Augustine learned after his mother died—but that death is "read" differently, interpreted differently in light of the resurrection faith.

This kind of assurance is not, in Augustine's view, merely an abstract thing. The conviction that life does not end with the dissolution of the body is an article of belief; but it is also more than that. It is also a reality that we experience, in part, in this life. Augustine gives Monica such a large place in this book because her life, and her approach to death, illuminate a variety of factors about the Christian life Augustine wants to communicate to his audience. Monica illustrates grace. She is a mother, a human symbol of God's gift of life. It is true that Augustine mostly thinks of grace in terms of what we would call "saving grace," but he also makes it clear throughout that existence itself is a gracious gift from God. His discussion of infants and pregnant women leads his readers to consider how God gives both grace and life through other creatures. But Monica, however much she gave Augustine in the flesh and spiritually, was by no means perfect; this allows her to be presented also as a recipient of grace and in this sense as a typical Christian.

Augustine tells us that as a child she had developed the habit of sipping wine when carrying the drink from the wine cellar for her parents. What began as a harmless wetting of the lips grew into gulping mouthfuls. Little Monica, however, was saved from this pit by a sarcastic remark on the part of an impertinent slave. The serving girl meant no good, only harm; and yet through her God acted for the good of her mistress. In another story that reveals the gap between our social world and theirs, Augustine tells how Monica would jokingly rebuke the women of the town when they complained about being beaten by their husbands. They should have realized that in assenting to their marriage vows, they were witnesses to their transformation into serving women who shouldn't defy their masters! Not our idea of marriage, perhaps; but in a world where marriage in many cases meant coming under the legal jurisdiction of your husband, one could argue that Monica was just being frank about the status of the woman. The battered faces of many wives testified to their unwillingness to hold their tongues in the face of their lord and master. Monica, cleverer than most, understood the woman's situation and developed a strategy both to avoid that scenario and to get her way. She never attempted to correct her husband immediately, but would wait until his anger subsided to work her ends.

Augustine goes to some pains to depict Monica's spiritual character, possessed by virtue of her relationship with God. He observes that she was at peace with her coming death and that she had a lofty disregard for the resting place of her mortal remains. This latter pleasantly surprised Augustine, because he knew that she had counted on being buried with her husband, mixed bag though he was, back in Africa. Monica's feeling of peace about this matter is clearly a sign of God's grace. He shows how her faith and confidence were rooted in an experience of the Divine Reality, by relating a vision that they were jointly given by God. This took place when they were staying in Ostia, the port city of Rome, in preparation for their voyage back to Africa. They were standing alone by a window, talking about the eternal life enjoyed by the saints. First they surveyed the joys provided by things of sense, and then they spoke of the nature of God's uncreated wisdom, realizing that understanding it lay at the furthest reaches of the human mind.

> So we were saying, if to anyone the commotion of the flesh were to fall silent; if the phantoms of earth, waters, and air were to fall silent; if the skies were to fall silent; if the soul itself were to fall silent within itself and pass beyond itself by not thinking about itself; if dreams, all the revelations of the imagination, every tongue, every signifying thing, and if everything that comes to be by the passing away of

something else would fall completely silent to anyone—since if anyone would hear them, all these
things would say, "we did not make ourselves, rather
did the one who dwells eternally make us"—this having been said, if they would now be quiet, since they
have roused the ear to the one who made them, God
alone would speak, not through them but through
Godself. Thus would it happen that we would hear
God's word, not through the tongue of the flesh, not
through the voice of an angel, not through the noise
from a cloud, not through the riddle of a parable, but
we would hear that very one whom we love in these
creatures, we would hear God apart from them. It
could happen in the same way as we ourselves are
now reaching out and in rapid thought have touched
upon the eternal wisdom that dwells over all things.

If this would continue, and if all other sights of a vastly unequal kind would withdraw themselves and this one sight would grab, absorb, and bury its audience in inner joys—would not the character of eternal life be like that moment of understanding for which we sighed in longing? (*Conf.* IX, 25–26)

Within five days of this vision, Monica was taken with a severe fever, losing consciousness at one point. When she briefly recovered her senses, she found Augustine and his brother hovering over her with great concern. Being somewhat disoriented, Monica asked where she was. The last minutes of her life reveal a religious peace that made her earlier elaborate preparations to be buried beside her husband irrelevant.

Then looking at us in our grief-stricken state she said, "lay your mother here." I was silent, holding back

tears; but my brother spoke something or other to the effect that she would not pass away in foreign parts but in her homeland, as if the fulfillment of that desire would make her happier. Having heard that, an anxious look crossed her face and she rebuffed him with her eyes for his thinking such things. Then she looked at me: "look what he's saying," she said, and shortly spoke to both of us. "Put this body any-where," she said, "don't let concern for it cause you any trouble at all. I ask only this of you: that you would remember me at the Lord's altar, wheresoever you be." And when she had clarified her meaning with these words, she became quiet in the struggle with her worsening sickness. (*Conf.* IX, 27)

The importance of this death-bed scene lies in the way Monica's right understanding of life and death led her to make fitting decisions. She had come to re-evaluate her ear-lier feeling that the happiness of an eternal life could some-how be supplemented by the happiness of having her mortal remains laid alongside those of her husband. That she had seen through what Augustine called this "vain notion" was a matter of rejoicing for him even in this time of grief.

The details of her passing, her funeral, and the grief felt by her son and grandson are likewise revealing, all provid-ing material for Augustine's analysis of the human situation. The certainty that Monica was going to a better place left Augustine worried about the meaning of what may seem to us to be very human feelings of mourning. It was under-standable that his son Adeodatus could not hold back his tears; but Augustine was troubled by his own inability to dismiss his sorrow in light of better knowledge. The impulse to weep filled him from the moment of Monica's death and did not depart from him until after the funeral, and after he had exhausted all efforts to stem the tide.

I closed her eyes, and a tremendous grief flowed into the outer regions of my heart and overflowed in tears. At the same moment, by a violent command of my mind, my eyes sucked up that fountain to the point of dryness. Such a struggle left me very badly off. When she let out her last breath, the boy Adeodatus broke out in sobs. Checked by all of us, he became quiet. In this manner something child-like in me, which had slipped into crying, was checked and quieted by the young voice of his heart. We didn't deem it appropriate to have a funeral with tearful moans and groans. For common custom has it that by these sounds some unhappiness on the part of those dying, or their total obliteration, is bemourned. But she neither had died unhappily nor was in all respects dying. We held this conviction on account of the witness of her habits, on account of her unfeigned faith, and grounded on sure reasons. What was it, then, that sorrowed so heavily within me but the fresh wound caused by the sudden breaking off of our very sweet and dearly beloved habit of living together? (*Conf.* IX, 29–30)

A constant strand of Augustine's thought concerns the weight of habit in our lives. Again and again he has recourse to this explanation to account for human behavior that otherwise makes no sense. Why didn't his parents have him baptized as a young boy to shield him from the sins of the teenage years? They followed the custom of deferring baptism to an age of maturity, so that the manifold sins of youth could be conveniently wiped out. Why were students permitted to carry out hazings and run wild at Carthage? No reason but long-standing custom. Why was Augustine so long unable to make a break from sexual relationships? A deeply entrenched habit held him fast by its constant and renewed pleasures. Generalizing from these experiences, Augustine attempts to attribute the power of grief to the breaking off of the pleasant habit of enjoying the company and life of those we love. This habit, then, is what leaves us so bereft at the death of those nearest and dearest to us.

The scene at Monica's death-bed is revealing. Once Adeodatus's cries are stifled, Evodius takes up the book of Psalms in chant, and the whole house gives the response: "Your mercy and Your judgment I will sing, O Lord" (Ps. 101:1). A large crowd of the faithful, men and women, gather around them, and preparations for the burial are made. Augustine is sequestered with comforters while his mother's body is washed and wrapped. Characteristically enough, Augustine attempts to say a few words fitting the occasion, which he later realizes were to assuage the torments he himself felt but was pretending not to feel in

front of the others. Inwardly, and in God's ears, he was berating himself for lacking perfect composure. He did achieve a semblance of control, but only for a moment. His feelings reasserted themselves so powerfully he had to admit what he was concealing. All that time he was secretly sorrowing in prayer to God, sorry that he felt so sorry. Upset by being subject to the necessities of our common lot, he was "torn by a two-fold sorrow, because in grieving I had created another grief." But not even when Monica was laid out for burial and the prayers were said did Augustine shed a tear. After the funeral, he went to the public baths, as he'd heard that the word "bath" comes from the Greek meaning "to cast away care." He bathes, he returns, he feels the same. Unable to route the grief in his heart, he decides to take a nap. Upon waking, he feels a little better and recalls the words of one of Ambrose's hymns. But that brings the feeling of Monica to life. Augustine thinks about how she prayed to God in tears for his salvation and broke down: "I let go the tears I was holding in, and out they flowed to the max, my heart pouring forth." He took respite in his tears and sorrow where only God could hear him.

CHAPTER TEN

Confessions without End

After the death of Monica, Augustine and companions returned to Africa with plans to live a quiet life devoted to the pursuit of wisdom, undistracted by the world. Augustine had no intention of replacing his worldly career with a job in Christian ministry—in fact, he tried quite consciously to avoid it. He simply wanted to do what he had been putting off for so long: really be a Christian. But events intervened to draw Augustine into the service of God, first as a priest and then as a bishop. He had stopped in the port city of Hippo and was attending church on Sunday. The bishop of Hippo was a Greek named Valerius.

Valerius had heard of Augustine, and he knew that he was a former professor of rhetoric and therefore an accomplished speaker. The bishop alerted the congregation to his presence that day. When the people saw him among them, they seized him and made him a presbyter (or priest) to assist their bishop. Being a Greek, Valerius's Latin was inadequate for the task of preaching, and he generally was not up to dealing with the many problems the church faced in Africa. Augustine was the perfect person for the job, forced though his ordination had been. Ambrose too had been impressed into the service of God in his manner, which was not unusual in the early centuries of the church. When Augustine wept on being thus compelled, the congregation assumed he was crying out of disappointment at not being appointed bishop! Nothing could be further from the truth. Augustine's dismay came rather from the fact that he knew his days of leisured study were over. He would spend the final forty years of his life in the ministry, becoming bishop of Hippo some four or five years later when old Valerius died. But when he was first ordained to the priesthood, Augustine thought himself too unversed in the church's books to do the job right. He requested and received a year's leave of absence, to study the Scriptures in preparation for his ministry.

> But can I ever with the tongue of my pen give an account of all Your encouragements and Your terrors, consolations and directives, by which You led me to preach Your word and dispense Your sacraments to Your people? For a long time I have been burning to meditate on Your law and to confess to You its knowledge—and my lack of expertise. I want to confess the beginning of Your illumination, and the remains of my shadows, until my weakness is consumed by Your strength. To no other purpose do I

want to apply the hours that flow by, the hours when I'm free from the necessities of replenishing the body and applying the mind, and free from the necessities of the service we owe human beings—and from what we do not owe but nonetheless pay. (*Conf.* XI, 2)

The *Confessions* records none of these further events in his life. Rather, in the remainder of the work, books X through XIII, Augustine explores a series of philosophical, theological and scriptural problems. This portion of the work is not minor; the length of books IX through XIII is approximately the same as the first eight books. These final four books of the work should not be conceived as a tagged-on ending or later addition. Some scholars have argued that the work originally ended with the conclusion of book IX, with Augustine's moving prayer for future generations to pray for his mother in fulfillment of her dying request. But there is a way to see this final section as integral to the whole work. Book X begins the departure from the autobiographical format and opens the more speculative part. The transition is a meditation on the act of confession and on the significance of the act of written confession. The final four books of the *Confessions* also discuss topics Augustine insinuated earlier in the autobiographical narrative. The seemingly endless questions of this final section highlight how the decisive conversion Augustine underwent was only a beginning in the life of grace. A brief summary of these final books makes this evident.

The tenth book opens by raising an issue that sheds light on the purpose of the work as a whole. Why make his confessions known in a written form, when the essential thing is for him to become transparent in his own self to God? Augustine's spirituality, however, has its social context and belongs to a life with communal goals. Being drafted into the church showed him this. Not for his own sake does Augustine make his life known; he wants to use it to illustrate his new understanding of God's grace. He envisions people out there who are like his former self: drawn to Christianity but weighed down with a sense of unworthiness and losing all hope of finding God.

> But O my private doctor, explain to me the point of my doing this sort of thing. When the confessions of my past evils . . . are read and heard, let them stir up people's hearts so they don't rest easily in their despair and say, "I can't do it." Rather, let their hearts arise in the love of Your mercy and in the sweetness of Your grace. For it is by grace that all the impaired, all who through grace become self-conscious of their own

impairment, receive power. And it delights good people to hear my past evils which they are presently without. It is not because these things are evil that it delights them, rather that they were evil and no longer exist. Is it then toward this goal, my Lord to whom my conscience daily confesses, more secure in the hope of Your mercy than in its own innocence—is it toward this goal, I ask, that I make my confession before You known through this writing to human beings as well? . . . This is the goal of my confessions, not to make known the sort of person that I was, but the sort of person I am. This is why I make this confession not only before You in a hidden exultation accompanied by trembling and in a hidden sorrow accompanied by hope, but also in the ears of humanity's believing sons and daughters, the comrades of my joy and the partners of my mortality. They are my fellow citizens and pilgrims, those who have gone before, those who follow, and the companions of my life. They are Your servants and my brothers, Your children whom You wanted to be my masters, whom You commanded me to serve if I want to live with You. (*Conf.* X, 4–6)

Augustine's writing of the *Confessions*, then, was part and parcel of the religious vocation to which God called him. It is one of the ways of putting his God-given gifts to work for the sake of the larger humanity, fellow travelers restless for God. The great inquiries into various problems that form the bulk of books X through XIII are also meant to be instructive for his audience, however much they also are a way-station of his mind's own road of ascent to God. Having confessed his love for God, he moves back to the question he has been circling through the whole work: What is God? This is not an abstract question as Augustine formulates it, but something quite concrete to any piety: "What is it I love when I love my God?" The point is that even after he has come into a definite relationship with God, the search goes on.

Books X through XIII of the *Confessions* are admittedly tough going. Often, when the *Confessions* is assigned at colleges, only the first nine books are read. But something is lost when this is done, because the thread of continuity between Augustine's attempted ascent to God, described in the autobiographical section, and the intellectual questionings of the last four books is very strong. The quest for knowing God involves bringing the self into question; and that process goes on throughout life, as "now we see through a glass, darkly" (1 Cor. 13:12 KJV). The continual inner exertion—intellectual, spiritual, and practical—is Augustine's prescription for the ills besetting our souls in this mortal life.

> So what do I love when I love my God? Who is the one above the top of my soul? Through my soul itself I will ascend to that one. I will go beyond that capacity of mine by which I adhere to the body and vitally replenish its structure. By that capacity I do not dis-

cover my God, for with that both a horse and a mule—to whom intellect is not present—would be able to discover God. That capacity is the same as the one by which even their bodies live. There is another capacity, by which I not only give life to my flesh but also bestow the power of perception upon it. . . . I

> will also go beyond this capacity of mine, for horses
> and mules have it as well: these too have the power of
> perception through the body. So I will go beyond this
> aspect of my nature, ascending by levels to the one
> who made me. And I come to the fields and broad
> quarters of memory. (*Conf.* X, 11–12)

Augustine renews his search for God through the mind,
but doing so requires an analysis of this instrument—his
mind—by which he knows God. The power of sensory
perception is clearly not the part of the mind capable of
knowing God, so he moves up to inquire about the nature
of the memory. This is the next logical stopping point, for
not only does memory contain the things his mother and
others told him about God as a child, but it is also his own
record of God's dealing with him. So too the Bible is a
kind of collective memory of the dealings of God with
humanity, however much it is shaped by faith. But Augustine's memory holds not only the things that have been
impressed on the mind by the senses—what he has heard,
what he has seen—but also all the ideas about God he had
entertained, both the false ones he has discarded and the
sound ones he has retained.

All this is not just a mental exercise. Augustine's search
for God is nothing other than the search for the happy life.
The questions he asks about the relation between God and
memory are then also posed regarding happiness. How is
it that in our search for the happy life, we expect to be able
to recognize it when we see it? Searching for it, we must
presently lack it; was there a time (prior to this life in the
body, Augustine hints) that we did possess it, so that we'll
know it when we see it? This and a variety of other problems pertaining to memory lead Augustine to the realiza-
tion that he doesn't possess anything like an adequate

knowledge of himself, let alone what God is. So he focuses on understanding the various powers of the mind with which human beings have been endowed.

Memory is key because it is the presupposition of there being a self at all. Although the word "self" does not have an exact equivalent in Augustine's Latin, the word can aptly be used to describe his view of the human person. By "self" we mean the unity of the various aspects of the human being. By remembering your past in the face of the future, you constitute whatever identity you have. When I head to work Monday morning and contemplate what I will do and be that day, I can do this only because I remember what I was the week before. And so on. But that moment, in which I'm unifying my past and future, is in the present! Strictly speaking, says Augustine, the past and the future do not exist, because we are always in the present. If our experience of the past and future always take place in a never-ending now, now, now, where each moment succeeds another and dies away—where is the unity of yourself? Its being seems limited to fragments of experience. This is why, for Augustine, the problem of memory leads to the problem of the self, which in turn leads to the problem of time.

This example of Augustine's philosophical musing is but a small sample of the profound reflections in book XI of the *Confessions*. Odd that this route would follow from his attempt to understand the Bible beginning with creation! If only Moses were here, Augustine wishes, he could ask what he meant by "beginning" in the first verse of the Bible. But what if Moses spoke only Hebrew? Then the sounds would beat his ears in vain. And how did God make the world by speaking? And so on. Augustine's relentless knocking at the door of Scripture and chasing questions arises in part out of his faith that through Scripture, God gives us understanding. Because of the depth of his questions, each of the last four books of the *Confessions* could profitably be read as a book in itself. Theology in the way that Augustine does it is "technical" in the sense that he tackles difficult issues at a relatively high level. He had been a professor for many years, after all.

> I will sacrifice to You my thinking and my tongue into slavery—give me what I might offer You. I am poor and have nothing; You are rich in all who call upon You, You who calmly put up with our worries. Circumcise my outer lips from all inner carelessness and lies. Your writings are my chaste delights: may I neither be deceived in them nor deceive from them. . . . O Lord make me whole and reveal them to me. See, Your voice is my joy, Your voice transcends a torrent of pleasures. Give me what I love, for You gave me that I would love. May Your gifts never leave me, may You not despise Your thirsty planting. I will confess to You whatever I should discover in Your books; I will

listen to the voice of praise. I will drink You and will meditate on the miracles of Your Law, from the beginning in which You made heaven and earth up until the eternal kingdom of Your holy city with You. (*Conf.* XI, 3)

Book XII of the *Confessions* is entirely devoted to the question of what the first two verses of Genesis mean. Early Christianity conceived Scripture to have an outer, "fleshly" meaning and an inner "spiritual" meaning. Many ancient biblical interpreters held there were three levels of meaning. The plain level is the historical sense (as when thus and such is said to occur); a second level involves a moral application; and the third level is meant to lead the mind up to an understanding of divine things. Augustine does not use our modern vocabulary (his book *A Literal Commentary on Genesis* does not equate the "literal" meaning with the "historical" one), but he treats Genesis as a bearer of multiple meanings. In this sense, he anticipated a central theme of recent currents in biblical interpretation. Where Augustine differs significantly from extreme post-modernism is in his firm belief in a reality behind the text. He reads the Bible because he is interested in something the text points to—or rather, because he is interested in the Reality expressing itself in and through the text.

This is Your word, which is also "the beginning," because it speaks in us. Thus it speaks in the flesh in the Gospel, and sounds outwardly to human ears to be believed and sought within in the eternal truth, where the only "good teacher" [Mark 10:17] instructs every disciple. There do I hear Your voice, O Lord, telling me that the one who teaches us is that one who speaks to us. (*Conf.* XI, 10)

Book XIII, the final book of the *Confessions,* positively bristles with unresolved questions. Augustine pursues the thought that "the heavens and the earth" God created first involved both a spiritual creation (heaven) and unformed matter (earth). This first, spiritual creation, he thinks is also signified in the words "let there be light." Clearly, he argues, a spiritual light is meant, because the sun and the moon were yet to be created. But the first elements of creation, the heaven and the earth created in the beginning (whatever they were) had no claim on God, nor offered God anything as a motivation for their creation. Thus, creation itself is a grace, an absolutely free act of God. What we mean by the term "created thing" or "creature" is simply that it is a dependent being: Its existence depends upon another; it is not its own cause. Augustine thus finds in the creation account a revelation of the nature of creaturely being and its relation to its creator. Far from conceiving Genesis as a blow-by-blow account of the creation of the world, he regards it a mystical text, whose mystery consists in the way it opens the understanding to multiple meanings. In this spirit, Augustine produces an allegorical reading of the various elements of creation enumerated in Genesis.

Underneath Augustine's persistent probing into both Scripture and reality is his conviction that God has created the mind and the world adapted to each other. The world has been founded on the same orderly (we would say, mathematical) basis as has the mind, or understanding. Although the mind is the greatest mystery of creation, far surpassing, for Augustine, the wonders of the physical universes, it can and must be explored. One reason for the "know thyself" imperative is that the mind is the site of temptations, many varieties of which he discusses in book X. But Augustine is careful to say that the demand to confess God is separate from the issue of whether one has a comprehension of a whole host of deep issues. One can confess God as Trinity without fully understanding what that means. Not that Augustine thinks he understands fully what it means to say that God is one reality and three persons; rather, he takes this as a task for Christian thought. The *Confessions* embarks on a line of thinking about God that Augustine will return to in one of his greatest later works, *On The Trinity*.

> Who understands the omnipotent Trinity? Yet who does not speak of it, if indeed they are speaking of it? Rare are the souls who know what they are talking about when they speak of the Trinity. People argue and struggle about it, although apart from peace, no one can have a vision of it. I wish that people would think about a triad in themselves. This triad is far from what we mean by the Trinity, but I'm suggesting that this is the place for working out, experimenting, and

thinking about that far off Triad. Now I'm talking about these three: to be, to know, and to will. For I exist, I know, and I will. Knowing and willing do I exist; and I know myself to exist and to will; and I want, or will, myself to exist and to know. So let those who are able see in these three how one life, one mind, and one existence are one inseparable life and cannot then be distinguished, the distinction being nonetheless real. (*Conf.* XIII, 12)

Created in the image and after the likeness of a trinitarian God, we are made to be with God, to love God, and ultimately to know God. As Augustine makes clear from the beginning, our loving God depends on our knowing God, if only by way of a dim presentiment. But even the slightest inkling of what God is suffices to make God loved by the soul. For the soul cannot rest in the many other loves it finds in the world, because the soul's love for things of the world reaches only finite things. Such loves can obviously not slake the thirst of the infinite in us, which loves the Infinite that is not only in us.

The *Confessions* exemplifies Augustine's thirst for the Infinite, his search for that which we see now only darkly in a mirror, but later face to face. He confesses the evils of his past, his unworthiness, so that his life would serve as a model for the work of grace. He hopes to encourage all who think that God comes only to the worthy to think again. The speculations into metaphysical questions of time and creation are also models for the Christian, models of the riches of knowledge out there for those who ask their questions in faith. The inquiry is carried on precisely as an open prayer to God, because otherwise such speculation would be pure audacity for a still-sinful soul with a recovering mind. Certainly there is biblical precedent: The apostle Paul prays for the Ephesians to receive "a spirit of wisdom and revelation in the knowledge of the Father" (Eph. 1:17). For Augustine this is not something that only an apostle can hope for—and with this sentiment and conviction, he concludes the *Confessions*.

> We, it is clear, see the things You have made because they exist; but they exist because You see them. We see outwardly that they exist, and inwardly that they are good; but You have seen to their having been made there, where You saw they were to be made. We have been moved at a certain time to doing good, after our heart had grasped it from Your Spirit. At an earlier time, we were moved to doing evil, while we were abandoning You. But You, God the one good, have never ceased from doing good. Even

the works of ours that are good are indeed Your gift, although they are not eternal. After they are done, we hope to take our rest in Your great sanctification. But You, a good that lacks no good—You are always at rest, because You are Your own rest. And what human being can grant another to understand this? What angel can grant it to an angel? What angel can grant it to a human being? Let it be asked of You, let it be sought in You, let there be knocking at your door—this, this is how it will be received, this is how it will be found, and this is how it will be opened. (*Conf.* XIII, 53)

CHAPTER ELEVEN

Career of the Bishop

As bishop of the church in Hippo, Augustine divided his daily routine between practical and contemplative activity. He spent mornings receiving people who brought their problems to the bishop, spiritual and financial, large and small. Afternoons were for his many writing projects, and he often had several going at once. Augustine also kept up the regimen of a monastic life. He had set up a monastery in the church garden and lived among his presbyters, the clergy working under him. They maintained rounds of prayer alongisde their regular duties.

Being a prolific author, he interlaced the practical life of a bishop with his writing activity. Many of his writings emerged from and were directed to specific situations that were troubling the church at the time. Augustine's earliest commentaries on biblical books—on Genesis and some Pauline letters—were intended as refutations of certain features of Manichean theology that he believed could be cleared up in light of the proper understanding of these scriptural books. But for all its importance at the time, this aspect of Augustine's work is perhaps the least relevant to our world. The Manichees and their fantastic cosmology have long ceased to have allure for Christians.

Other aspects of Augustine's work as a bishop have greater relevance to theological, psychological, and social problems of today. Without attempting to bring into view the full scope of his career in the church, or the many problems he sought to deal with in his preaching and teaching, let us take a look at Augustine the controversialist. We will consider three major theological controversies that occupied his attention for almost four decades. The first of these—the Donatist Controversy—concerns his attempts to unify the orthodox churches in Africa into the Catholic fold. A schism in the church had begun during a time of persecution and was still unhealed when he was ordained. The second controversy—against pagans who blamed Christianity for the fall of Rome—issued in what is probably Augustine's most famous book after the *Confessions: The City of God*. Third, there is the Pelagian Controversy, famous as a debate on the freedom of the will. Augustine and Pelagius, two Christians of decidedly ascetic convictions, each developed persuasive but incompatible theories about the relation between the human will and divine grace in the process of salvation.

The Donatist Controversy—actually a schism in the churches of Roman Africa—was the first item on Augustine's

agenda when he was made presbyter of the church at Hippo. Valerius, the aging bishop of Hippo, had hoped that the ex-rhetor impressed into his service would be an effective point-man against the Donatist Church. The Donatist Church was more powerful and numerous in much of Africa than the Catholic one. But who and what were the Donatists? The name comes from their bishop Donatus, who was the second bishop of the schismatic church in Carthage. Congregations separate from the Catholics had for some time now been well-established throughout Africa. The origins of the schism lay in events dating back to the last of the pagan per-secutions of the church, the so-called Great Persecution of 303–305. The trouble began when the Catholic bishop of Carthage died and three local bishops hastily ordained a man named Caecilian, all prior to the arrival of a larger body of bishops from the outback. This hasty and calculated move deprived these other bishops of their rights to participate in the very important choice of bishop for the capital of Roman Africa. They were deeply affronted. To make matters worse (and this was the true cause of the Donatist schism), one of the three bishops, the infelicitous Felix who participated in the ordination of Caecilian, was suspected of handing over holy books to the authorities during the persecution. This was, of course, strictly forbidden and regarded as a heinous sin, almost as bad as idolatry, because it meant not only cooperating with the persecutors but also betraying the Lord. The late-arriving bishops regarded the ordination of Caecilian as invalid, because they believed Felix had corrupted his office and thus had lost the ability to carry it out. Behind their rigorist attitude lay the long history of the churches in Africa, where the most important thing had been resisting paganism and maintaining the church pure from the taint of the pagan world. Such purity, they held, was the condition under which God would guarantee the grace of the sacraments. A bishop who had been defiled by polluting contact with idolatry could not be a vehicle of God's grace. These bishops, therefore, took the bull by the horns and ordained a person who in their eyes would be a legitimate bishop, a man named Majorinus. Majorinus was not long for this world, however; and upon his death those dissenting bishops ordained another, Donatus, who held the bishop's seat at Carthage for thirty years.

Although a majority of African Christians recognized Donatus as the legitimate bishop, the Catholics continued with the bishop they had ordained in Carthage. As a matter of course, he presided in forthcoming years over the ordination of various bishops and priests throughout Africa. But in the eyes of the party of Donatus, these ordinations were illegitimate, because they all depended for their office upon a man whose own ordination was indelibly faulty. The fact that a later imperial investigation determined that Felix did not hand over sacred books did nothing to relieve the situation. Things had already gone too far: The African cities and towns had two parallel church structures, each claiming to be the true "catholic," or universal, church and the remnant of true believers.

Both sides made various attempts to get the church at Rome and the emperor to resolve the matter in their favor. After a long series of appeals, hearings, and investigations, the bishop of Rome, various councils of bishops, and the emperor Constantine came down on the Catholic side. Despite the emperor's promulgation of a severe edict against the schismatic party, which ordered the confiscation of its churches and the exile of its leaders, the Donatist church survived and even established dominance in large parts of Africa by the time Augustine was made a priest. The majority of African Christians (largely poor farmers who still associated imperial authority with persecutions of the church) may have found the Donatist claims convincing, because they appeared to be more in keeping with the ideals of holiness and integrity that had been the hallmarks of the African church from its beginnings.

In light of this situation, Augustine had a real job on his hands. He went at it with all the vigor of a convert, holding that God's grace, and not human purity, validated the church and its sacraments. For his own part, he had come to believe that one of the most important aspects of a single universal church was that it was God's way of ensuring a correct transmission of the truth. This truth had been entrusted by Jesus to the apostles, and then from the apostles to the first bishops, and from them to their successors. Because it was largely a matter of winning the hearts and minds of the common people over to the Catholic side, Augustine debated Donatist leaders who had the courage to engage in public discussion with a former rhetor. He also picked up some of his opponents' tactics, turning their weapons against them. The Donatists had

been adept at putting their theology into songs for the common people; Augustine responded in kind, composing an alphabetical song against them in a popular rhythm.

> ABOUNDING sins are throwing believers in turmoil . . .
> BEST listeners ask who tore the net the Lord hauled in full of all sorts . . .
> CARETAKER, our great God, You can free us from these false prophets . . .
> DECLARED our forefathers the facts of the case and wrote them down. . .
> EVIDENT it is how good and pleasant for brothers and sisters to live as one . . .
> You who rejoice in peace, just admit what's true!
> (*Alphabetical Psalm Against the Donatists* 8–73, freely adapted)

The process of reclaiming Africa for the Catholic party was greatly aided by a major organizing effort of the bishop. Augustine enlisted some of his friends—Alypius, for instance, who had become bishop of Thagaste. With the help of other highly trained men experienced in the imperial service, the tide began turning against the Donatists. Yet despite the best efforts, a clean sweep of Africa could not be made by verbal persuasion alone. Both sides had resorted to tactics of intimidation that included violence and terror. Then, imperial troops were brought into Africa to shut down Donatist churches and force their congregations into the Catholic basilicas. Augustine had initially opposed the use of force. He had been firmly convinced that persuasion was the only appropriate means for religious truth to win out. But later, when an ex-Donatist admitted to him that he would never have entered the Catholic fold apart from that act of imperial coercion, Augustine began to think the action justified. After all, hadn't God used a combination of sweet persuasion and fear to convert him? (And hadn't he himself learned his first lessons at school under the compulsion of the master's rod?) With an interpretation that makes many Augustine scholars today wince, Augustine took the biblical phrase "compel them to enter" (Luke 14:23) about bringing in uninvited guests to a wedding banquet and applied it to the coercion of the Donatists.

The power of the state broke the back of the Donatist church in Africa, but could not completely eradicate it. Deeply rooted in the loyal religious sensibilities of peasant farmers, Donatist churches remained in the more remote areas until the Arab conquests made conversion to Islam a lively option. The fact that other Christians in areas overrun by the seventh-century Arab conquest resisted the pressure to convert to Islam suggests that the Donatists' loyalty to Christ had been undermined by centuries of harassment by the Catholic church and the powers of the state.

Let us turn now to Augustine's second great controversy, the one behind his biggest book. The complete title Augustine gave it reveals what kind of book it is: *The City of God against the Pagans.* This voluminous work (twenty-two "books") is an "apology," a genre of writing used by ancient pagan and Christian authors. The *Apology* of Socrates, or the apologies of Christian writers such as Justin Martyr or Tertullian, are all responses (the Greek word "apology" means: a response). The early Christian "apologists" were trained intellectuals hitting back at negative conceptions of their religion, responding to the bad rap pagans were giving Christianity. Augustine, for his part, felt compelled to answer the pagans who charged that the fall of Rome was due to the abandonment of the traditional Roman gods that had made the Empire great. This charge was only part of what came his way in the aftershock of a barbarian invasion of Italy that breached the famous walls of Rome.

It is perhaps not out of order to mention that the fall of Rome is not quite what it sounds like. Historians have long acknowledged that the Roman Empire did not simply "fall." Only the western half of the Roman empire fell, beginning in the early fifth century. For both military and administrative purposes, the empire had been divided in the late third century. The emperor then took a junior colleague who ruled with him, one over the Latin West and the other over the Greek East. Shortly thereafter, Constantine established a second capital for the eastern part. Constantinople (present-day Istanbul) had its imperial court, a newly created senatorial order of its own, and an imperial residence. The eastern half, or Byzantine Empire as we know it, actually lasted until the fifteenth century, when the Ottoman army finally took the city. Italy was overrun by a variety of Germanic tribes from the fifth century onward, but at that time the city of Rome was only the symbolic center of the empire. The western capital, where the western emperor resided, had long since moved from Milan and from there to Ravenna. By the mid-fifth century, however, there ceased to be any western Roman Empire, because a German king, Odoacer, unseated the last western emperor, Romulus Augustulus, in 476. Germanic warlords took the place of the western Roman emperor from then on and ruled over a mixed regime of Romans and their own peoples.

The fall of the city of Rome to the Visigoths in 410 was the event that set Augustine into motion writing *The City of God*. This fall was more than a symbolic shock, however: Waves of Roman refugees fled to Africa. The unthinkable had happened, and the question was, "how could it have happened?" Pagans pointed an accusing finger at Christianity. Could it be a coincidence, they asked, that Rome's walls stood impregnable so long as the old gods received their due worship? Could it be coincidence that Rome was ravaged by greedy hordes only after the Christian emperors had refused to halt the Christians' demand to destroy the ancient temples and their sacred images? The gods of Rome had made Rome great. Rome had been severely threatened in the late third century, but she had come through, thanks to the firm hand of an experienced soldier who respected the ancestral forms of piety. Their argument was that Rome had been corrupted from within by Christianity, a religion foreign to all and native to none. Augustine opens his *magnum opus* by stating the problem:

> Most glorious is the city of God, no matter whether
> we consider it in the course of these times when it is

on pilgrimage amongst the wicked and living by faith, or as it is in the stability of its eternal seat which we now await patiently, "until justice be turned to judgment" [Ps. 94:15]. Then will justice take hold preeminently, with final victory and total peace. I have taken up the task of defending the city of God against those who to the city's founder prefer their own gods. I owe the inception of this task to you, my beloved son Marcellinus, and to my promise to you to defend her. It is a big and difficult task, but God is our helper. For I know what resources it takes to persuade the proud how great the power of humble lowliness is . . . But humility's height towers over all by the grace bestowed upon it. For the God and Founder of the city we have set out to discuss has given in writing to his people an opening in a verse of the divine law, where it says "God resists the proud, but gives grace to the humble" [I Pet. 5:5]. This is truly said by God. (*City of God*, I, 1)

"City" is a potent symbol, for it is everything that epitomizes the human. A city means people living so densely that a different way of life comes into being, giving rise to all that we associate with culture: art, music, poetry. Of course, culture is not merely these. The recently popularized notion of "pop culture" is actually a redundancy, based on a mistaken view that only "high culture" is culture. When Augustine talks about a city (better translated here as "society"), his attention is on politics and ideology as they are expressed in literature, history, and religion. In *The City of God,* Augustine squares off with Roman patriotism, which was an ideology of empire. He attacks the theology of pagan religion, which was an essential element of that ideology. The goals of Rome he sees to be the goals of all human civic association after the fall: worldly glory, pleasure, and power. Augustine calls the kind of society based around those goals "the earthly city," of which the Roman empire is merely the latest example. Many of the goods of that city are worthwhile, for various human goals, and are therefore desirable. The problem is that these goods are limited and finite, because the resources for their production are finite. Thus there will never cease to be strife over these goods, for their level of worth is often determined by their scarcity. The rich and powerful will be few and will necessarily oppress the many, who are poor. This is the nature of rule in the earthly city, according to Augustine.

The City of God, on the other hand, is based around a good of a different kind: an eternal good that can be enjoyed by all with prejudice to none and plenty for all. Christians are pilgrims in the world of the earthly city but are true citizens of the heavenly city along with its other inhabitants, the holy angels. However, while we are on pilgrimage, even when we are members of the universal church, the City of God's representative on earth, we can never be exactly sure which of our fellow pilgrims really belong to that city. Augustine didn't believe that God sorted out the wheat from the tares, or the goats from the sheep, in this life. The church was not just composed of the righteous and the holy. It was, as he said in a memorable phrase, "a mixed bag" (*corpus permixtum*). This follows from the theology of the church Augustine developed against the Donatists, in part by borrowing from a notable Donatist theologian. Augustine conceives the church as a hospital of sorts, a first aid station for the wounded on the

way to the great sorting out. The church takes in all comers, whatever their ultimate ends may be.

> I have categorized the human race into two sub-species: one consists of those who live according to human standards and the other of those who live according to God. We also refer to them in a mystical fashion as two cities, that is, two societies of human beings, one of which is predestined to rule with God for eternity, the other to undergo eternal punishment with the Devil. (*City of God*, XV, 1)

Predestination does not entail, as many have fearfully imagined, that God winds us up like mechanical toys, with some destined to wander off a cliff and others programmed to reach the city of bliss. For the will by which sinners sin is none other than their own, not some alien will forcing them to sin against their better intentions and desires. Augustine conceives human beings to be locked into their own sinful habits, saved from them only by God's grace. God initiates the process of salvation and makes human beings just, which Augustine thinks we cannot achieve on our own. Some of his ancient readers wondered whether human beings would be responsible to maintain righteousness in view of this theory. His answer, in brief, is that we are responsible to do right (for no one ever forces us to do wrong); but only by God's continued action upon us would we ever be consistent and persevere in the new life of grace. What then of those whom God has not predestined to receive grace and persevere in it? They are not, for Augustine, in any sense doomed against their wills; rather they are doomed because of their wills. God's foreknowledge of their destiny did not cause their eternal destruction; that is the work of sin in them (that is, their sinful wills) and is in no wise attributable to God. Luther, Calvin, and other Protestant Reformers followed Augustine's lead in insisting on the hard teaching of predestination. They saw it as the consistent conclusion of the teaching that God's grace is absolutely unmerited and the sole cause of salvation.

Despite the way Augustine regards predestination as a teaching that applies both to individuals and to the collectivities created by like-minded individuals, the "political theology" that emerges from *The City of God* is not a recipe for a theocracy, a holy nation run by saints. There is a human city in which Christians may rule, but that is a perilous job. Not only is Christianity transnational for Augustine, and thus beyond the claims of any one nation, but it is also concerned with a different good and a different justice from that of any earthly state. Earthly rule inherently involves injustice, even when it tries to have a good system of justice. The most a Christian ruler can do is ameliorate the harshness of the conflict of interests that is at the basis of all civic existence. The man to whom the *The City of God* was dedicated, Flavius Marcellinus, was an Imperial commissioner at Carthage but also a member of the church. Unfortunately for him, an attempted coup on the part of a general named Heraclian cast suspicion upon him; and when the coup d'etat was suppressed, Marcellinus was sentenced to death. All the machinery of the church was set in motion to obtain a pardon from the emperor. Augustine himself hoped that mercy would triumph over what passed for justice. Alas, heads must roll in the earthly city, and Marcellinus lost his. This was a bitter lesson for Augustine: He abandoned the remnants of his previous enthusiasm for what a Christian emperor could achieve by way of justice. Christian emperors and Christian officials and soldiers, he concluded, "had" to do a lot of things that Christians ought not to do.

Augustine's pessimism about the limits of human attempts to achieve earthly justice reflects his own experience of the Roman Empire, which was a military dictatorship. On the other hand, his view is part and parcel of the way he defines the nature of the two cities having disparate purposes: temporal goods versus eternal goods. Because the earthly city by definition refers to human communities that are built around the love of the goods of the earthly life, no particular earthly society, even if composed largely of Christians—say, the Roman Empire or the U.S.A.—can be identified with the City of God. Augustine doesn't believe that the events of our own history can be read as clearly as the events of Scripture. There can be no "Redeemer Nation" in Augustine's theology, because there already is a redeemer—Christ—and a redeemed people, the human citizens of the City of God. All nations, as we use

the word, are "under God" in the sense of being within God's general providence, but no nation is of God. God's people, rather, have their minds set on a different kind of city with a categorically different kind of love. The two cities are distinct in their goals because they are distinct in their origins, ends, and inhabitants. One contains fallen angels, and the other the angels that never fell; both contain human beings.

> Two kinds of love, therefore, created two kinds of cities. The love of oneself, to the point of disregard of God, has obviously created the earthly city; the love of God, to the point of disregard of self, has indeed created the heavenly city. In brief, the former glories in itself, but the latter in God. (*City of God*, XIV, 28)

In his social analysis, as in his view of the individual, love is key. Expressed more precisely, what is loved is key to the shape that our lives—both individual and collective—take. The kinds of things we love, and how we love them, make us the kind of beings we end up being. The generality of this insight does not diminish its profundity when applied either to politics or psychology. Precisely because the earthly city's principle is self-love, our attempts to do justice in earthly matters are opposed not just by demonic forces of destruction without. The human tendencies toward self-love and self-protection can also blind us to our own injustices in the very pursuit of justice itself.

We come now to Augustine's third big controversy: the role of the human will in salvation. It was initiated by Pelagius, a British monk who was among the many refugees who fled Italy from the Visigothic invasion. He was already a noted Christian teacher, housed, as was customary, among one of the best families of the now largely Christian Rome. Ascetic teachers like Pelagius sometimes made spectacular conversions among the aristocracy, often among the women. This could and did result in enormous fortunes of land being given to the church. Aristocratic families, particularly their women, were often drawn to rigorous forms of Christianity. There were strict regimens of prayer, diet, clothing, sex, and sleep, all of which involved strenuous exertion without demanding the total renunciation of property. A threat to their properties, ironically, indirectly brought about the Pelagian Controversy.

At the first rumble of barbarian hoofbeats, many of the powerful Christian families of Rome fled to their bountiful estates in Sicily or Africa. Traveling in their train, Pelagius passed through Africa on his way to Palestine and narrowly missed encountering Augustine. One of Pelagius's disciples, however, a man named Caelestius who had made an impressive conversion with full renunciation, did come to Carthage. There he began propagating his master's ascetic theology. Augustine was not the only great theologian around, and not everybody agreed with everything he said. Pelagius, for one, had read the *Confessions* and was not altogether pleased with elements of Augustine's theology of grace—and he did not conceal his feelings about it. Caelestius had come to Africa spoiling for a fight.

What had especially irritated Pelagius was the sentiment Augustine expressed in a prayer found in book X of the *Confessions:* "Give what You command and command what You will." This struck Pelagius as gruel for the pusillanimous soul. He had been accustomed to serving a stiffer, more bracing course. But Pelagius by no means denied grace, as is sometimes falsely alleged; rather his conception of it was different from Augustine's. Grace for him included all that God gave us in creation, all of which enabled us to carry out the divine commands. Pelagius's basic take was that God didn't give commands that were impossible to perform. Had not God given us a free will to do the good which is apparent to our God-given mind? And had not God given sufficient commands to make His will known? Hadn't God given us the teachings and example of Christ? Ungrateful creatures to go on whining about our weaknesses and begging for more grace when what we really needed was to jolly well get on with our part in salvation— doing the right thing! Augustine begged to disagree:

> One must oppose in the sharpest and most forceful fashion those who say that without the help of God the strength of the human will can either maintain perfect justice or make progress toward it by exerting

an effort. When pressed how they would presume to assert that this happens without divine assistance, they back off and do not dare give utterance to the expression, as they see how irreligious and intolerable it is. But they go on to say that the reason such things don't come about without divine assistance is that God created humanity with free choice of the will, and that God teaches how one ought to live by giving ethical guidelines. They claim God certainly does help, to the extent of eliminating human ignorance, so people would know what ought to be avoided and what ought to be sought in their actions. By these means one would, through an innately implanted power of free choice, merit the attainment of a life both happy and eternal. This happens by setting forth on the proven path and living in a self-controlled, just, and religious way. Now we say that the human will is aided in doing justice as follows. Beyond the fact that human beings were created with a free will, beyond God's teaching as the means by which one learns how to live right, we receive the Holy Spirit by which there arises in our mind a delight in and love of that highest and unchangeable Good which is God. (*The Spirit and the Letter,* II, 4–III, 5)

Augustine did not disagree with Pelagius concerning *what* constituted salvation but about *how* one attains it. Like Pelagius, Augustine sought to impress his congregations with the need for greater holiness in life. The habit of peppering one's speech with oaths needed to be broken; married people needed to work at maintaining fidelity to each other; everyone needed to strive to curb their own selfishness and maintain as much justice as possible in their earthly affairs. There was room all over for improvement; but the debate was about how people could move toward the transformation of life called for by the Gospel. Augustine's fear was that because Pelagius emphasized so much the gifts of God in the creation of human beings, the grace of Christ and the Holy Spirit were somehow being given short shrift. As we know from the *Confessions,* Augustine was gung-ho about the notion that whatever exists is to some extent good, insofar as existence itself is good. He did not want to diminish the great gifts of God to human beings in creation, but he worried about what had become of those gifts throughout the course of human history. For human history, even if it is Christianly understood as the history of salvation, is also the history of sin—both individual and collective— and the history of the accumulation and encrustation of sin.

> Human nature was indeed originally created faultless and without any defect. But the human nature by which each and everyone is born from Adam now stands in need of a doctor, because it is not healthy. All the goods which human nature has in its forma- tion—life, the senses, mind—it has from its creator and maker. But the defect which casts a shadow on and weakens these natural goods (such that our nature has need of enlightening and healing) is not derived from its author who cannot be faulted. Rather does the defect derive from the original sin which was committed by a free choice. (*On Nature and Grace,* III, 3)

To Augustine, we have been hobbled, blinded, and beaten silly by sin; but this is not just the result of our own personal sins. He developed the concept of original sin to deal with the complexity of the situation. Now, the term "original sin" is not found as such in the Bible. The con- cept is rather an interpretation of the creation and fall story. Looking at the story of how sin and all its woe entered the world, it's not hard to see the basis for this

interpretation. One sad tale in Genesis follows another with an air of apparent inevitability: The first sin is followed by the first homicide, brother killing brother. Violence becomes the rule altogether; God regrets what has become of the creation and decides to try again, but even the sons of that righteous man Noah cannot contain the inclination to sin.

The theological doctrine of original sin claims that later sins are significantly different from the first, because they were committed under decidedly worse conditions. When the first human couple, "favored of heaven so highly" (as Milton has put it), was moved "to fall off from their Creator, and transgress his will," there were not many exonerating circumstances. They lived in a garden of earthly delights, with only the minor obligation of light custodial duties imposed upon them. They needed merely to tend the garden; their food grew of its own

211

accord. After the curses God put on the land and the penalties on Adam and Eve, life became a lot tougher—and people did too. They had become—in Augustine's view—damaged goods.

In the case of sophisticated creatures like human beings, "damaged goods" means a lessening of the goods that were originally given. Augustine thinks our faculties are actually damaged and so rendered less effective in their functioning. The intellect and the will are our organs, so to speak, for the good, for knowing and willing the good. The God-given faculties Pelagius would have us rely on are not what they once were. The disruption of our faculties in their orientation toward the good throws us into disarray, generally incited by the multiplicity of lesser loves that

come into view and urge us on. Even in our attempts to do good, we do wrong: our systems of justice are not clean from the death of the innocent and the torture of the guilty. Collectively and individually we need healing, and we have need—Augustine loved to say—of a doctor.

> Any free choice, if the way of truth be hidden, lacks power for anything but sinning. Even when what is to be done and the aim of ethical striving have begun to be unhidden, unless it provides delight and is loved, it is not done, it is not embraced, and one does not live well. But that it would be loved, "the love of God is shed abroad in our hearts"—not through the free choice which arises from us—but "through the Holy Spirit which is given to us" [Rom. 5:5]. (*The Spirit and the Letter*, III, 5)

The "way of truth" can be hidden in many different fashions. It is possible, as Augustine's biography witnesses, to hear the way of the truth in an external way without really knowing the truth. Even after Augustine had elected to renew his status as a catechumen in the Catholic church, he remained in shadows that needed to be swept away by the bright light of understanding that comes from above with a life-changing manifestation. This is what makes for conversion. Although the idiom of our language insists on putting us in the active mode (we "convert"), Augustine's description and language suggests rather that we are converted. What converts us is love, and what is converted—turned—in us is love, or rather all our loves. Pelagius's view didn't make sense to Augustine when he thought about inner human experience generally, or the experience of the sacraments, which for him give us something, bestow something real upon us. Augustine (and later Roman

Catholic theology) distinguishes between the guilt of original sin (which is actually remitted by the act of baptism) and the penalty for it, which lives in our members. So even though baptism eliminates the first, our punishment remains with us in this life—and for some, afterwards as well. God's punishments correlate with the damages we have inflicted on ourselves. The shackles we have forged prevent us from truly being ourselves, from being the creatures we were created to be. This happens on the level of both the individual and society. We are hamstrung by our histories: Those that weigh us down personally are interwoven with those that beset the larger culture. And this hampering effect of accumulated sin can coexist with our best intentions—and sometimes exists because of them. Augustine's fierce opposition to the Pelagian position arises from his deep sense that with damage so grave, we need a boost from beyond.

Pelagius himself undoubtedly meant well. His Christian commitment and activity, practical and scriptural, are not to be questioned. Scholars have for some time now recognized that the term "heretic" ill befits him, however much the great controversy carried on against him and his followers has branded him that. Augustine was relentless in his prosecution of the case against anyone who defended "Pelagian" views. He became positively crotchety when a new champion for the other side, a learned bishop named Julian, suggested that Augustine's conception of original sin contained residues of his Manichean past. All the means of enforcing orthodoxy that Augustine and the African bishops had developed against the Manicheans and Donatists were now marshalled, and Julian was exiled to the eastern parts of the empire.

C O N C L U S I O N

A great sense of wonder comes over me about this, amazement takes hold of me. People go around marveling at high mountains, the immense waves of the sea, the very wide flow of rivers, the size of the ocean, and the orbits of the stars—and they leave themselves out of the picture. They don't marvel about the fact that although I am speaking of all these things I am not seeing them with my eyes, nor would I be speaking of them unless I had seen them within. The mountains, waves, rivers, and stars which I have seen and the ocean which I have believed to exist, I have seen in my memory in such immense spaces it is as if I were seeing them outside. (*Conf.* X, 15)

Climbing a mountain one day, an Italian poet of the fourteenth century opened his pocket-size copy of Augustine's *Confessions* and was seized with a sense that his priorities were wrong, all wrong. Petrarch had hit upon a passage where Augustine is puzzling about the way people wander far and wide to see the marvels of nature and yet have no sense of the marvelous power within, the power by which they see and recall the marvels their eyes have seen. Augustine's insight into the miraculous nature of the mind and the human person is an area where he needs to be heard anew today. His manner of thinking about the self is a refreshing break from current, technical ways of talking about human beings (many forms of psychology, philosophies of mind, socio-biology, and so on). Such "scientific" systems evade the personal dimension that alone forces us to be real to ourselves and to others. In a word, they are insufficiently confessional.

Confession emerges as a prime element of Augustine's thought precisely because it is an activity essential to being a self. The very act of confession involves self-awareness on the part of the person engaged in confessing. For Augustine, the human mode of being—a conscious mode of being as opposed to purely animal forms—is an existence fraught with the basic tension inherent in being a creature, finite and temporal but created in the image of God. This means that an essential element of what we are depends upon what God and God's image are. From this arises the demand for both self-knowledge and knowledge of God. This connection is why Augustine links scriptural ways of thinking of God with the philosopher's quest for self-knowledge. Created in the image of God, we are constituted to be ourselves most fully when we are in God. Being created entities, however, our existence cannot be the same as God: We perish and go. In our lifetime, an age of partial separation from God, we are in the flesh, which refers not only to our physicality, but also to the limits of our capacity for knowledge. Thus for Augustine, as later for Calvin, self-knowledge cannot be attained apart from the knowledge of God—and only God can bestow it. Divine grace alone imparts the illumination that conveys true knowledge.

But it is not just upon the structures of knowledge that sin has crashingly fallen. The inheritance of original sin infects the natural desires in us and inflames them, making resistance well-nigh impossible. Ignorance compounds the problem. Both mind and will conspire against our better selves. Our capacities for action, both personal and collective, are limited and corrupted by how we conceive the matters demanding our action. By no means are our capacities for thought and action totally separate; on the contrary, they are intimately linked. Augustine was very fond of a biblical image for this aspect of human existence: We are blinded in our sins—and our blindness is such that we don't even know we're blind! This is because we are always seeking to exonerate our life and our point of view rather than accusing ourselves of our sins. The healing that grace accomplished heals us so that we can see and confess our sins, and so be turned.

Augustine offers a profound understanding of the human person. The self is thoroughly social, yet individuals are irrevocably drawn into a relationship with God, be it positive or negative. Within its inner space, its subjectivity, the human self finds itself split apart into the moments of time that constitute experience. Therefore we are haunted by the sense of never being quite complete. Indeed, the human self by itself is incomplete. And that is where God comes in—or rather, is there always, because that is the way God "is": always. The human self, which lacks its own unity, can find unity only in light of God's unity. And God's unity—Augustine discovered in his conversion and life as a bishop—is made available to human beings in a human form: first in Christ and second in the church. For the church is the social "within" of Christian existence, the space for working out our salvation.

Further Reading

All the translations of Augustine have been my own, including the biblical passages found in his works. I have utilized the Latin text of the *Confessions* given by James J. O'Donnell of the University of Pennsylvania in his superb commentary, *Augustine, Confessions* (3 volumes, Oxford University Press, 1992). For other writings of Augustine, I have translated from the Latin of the standard critical editions. Occasionally I have cited other biblical translations (King James Version and New Revised Standard Version) and have credited them in the text. Biblical quotations in passages from Augustine have been noted parenthetically, but I have not signalled his every verbal allusion to the Bible, because these are far too numerous.

My understanding of Augustine has been almost two decades in the making, beginning with my graduate studies at Union Theological Seminary and Columbia University under Richard A. Norris Jr. and continuing through my engagement with the voluminous writings of and scholarship on the bishop of Hippo. Of scholars writing in English, two must be named in whose debt I especially stand: Peter Brown, whose magisterial biography, *Augustine of Hippo: A*

Biography (University of California Press, 2000), has recently been re-released with an update in the form of an epilogue; and Henry Chadwick, one of the foremost authorities on Augustine and early Christianity. To readers interested in reading the *Confessions,* I recommend Chadwick's excellent translation (with informative introduction and notes) published by Oxford University Press in its World's Classics series. I have taught this translation so much since its appearance, that I may have borrowed phrases inadvertently from Chadwick here and there (perhaps there are also traces of the fine translation by R. C. Pine-Coffin, published by Penguin Books [1961], or the beautiful seventeenth-century rendering by William Watts [reprinted in the Loeb Classical Library]). Chadwick has written an introductory book, *Augustine: A Very Short Introduction* (Oxford University Press, 1986), which is excellent for readers who are interested in Augustine's life and thought but are daunted by the thickness of the aforementioned work by Peter Brown. Brown's biography of Augustine is such a fine read that I hesitate to offer other suggestions for introductory reading. Both these works contain more than enough suggestions for further reading. A treasury for Augustine study is *Augustine Through the Ages: An Encyclopedia,* ed. Allan D. Fitzgerald (Grand Rapids: Wm. B. Eerdmans Publishing Co., 1999), featuring articles by experts and an important bibliography.

I would also be remiss here to fail to indicate the debts I owe to many Augustine scholars hailing from a great number of countries (the United States, Canada, Great Britain, Ireland, France, Germany, Belgium, The Netherlands, Austria, Switzerland, Italy, and Algeria). My understanding of Augustine has benefited considerably from the works of these experts over the years.

Index

Index